"*Children of the Aging Self-Absorbed* fills an important niche in the self-help literature: dealing with aging, difficult, narcissistic parents and grandparents. The book is a guide for adult children of such parents, and offers much wisdom. Brown delineates four types of self-absorbed parents—Clingy, Suspicious-Defensive, Arrogant, and Belligerent—and provides excellent strategies for managing interactions with each type of parent. The book has useful exercises designed to help readers manage their side of these very difficult relationships more effectively. The overriding message is that the adult child must—and can—let go of hoping to change the parent and instead develop self-protective coping behaviors. This book is a good resource for anyone dealing with an aging self-absorbed parent or grandparent, as well as for therapists helping their clients in such situations."

> —**Eleanor F. Counselman, EdD, ABPP, CGP, LFAGPA**, president-elect of the American Group Psychotherapy Association, and assistant clinical professor of psychiatry, Harvard Medical School

"Nina Brown lights the way, helping you navigate the roller coaster of caring for narcissistic, aging parents and grandparents. This groundbreaking book introduces valuable exercises and practical advice to strengthen your resilience and protect you from taking in the negativity of your self-absorbed parents."

> —**Ann Steiner, PhD, MFT, CGP, FAGPA**, faculty of The Psychotherapy Institute, board member of the American Group Psychotherapy Association, and author of *How to Create and Sustain Groups that Thrive*

"This new text by Nina Brown makes clear the impact of self-absorbed parents and offers some useful techniques about what to do about them.... Written in an easily accessible and commonsense tone, [*Children of the Aging Self-Absorbed* has] something to offer for those with relatively little background in psychology and human development theory, as well as those with considerable experience.... Brown takes the reader through the basics of coping with a problem that is faced by a good deal of the early, middle, and later adult population.... This text is a useful and practical review of the issues involved with parent-child dynamics in the adulthood years and provides some solid structure for describing, categorizing, and responding to these issues in an effective manner."

—**Joshua M. Gross, PhD, ABPP, CGP**, psychologist and
    director of group programs at The University Counseling
    Center at Florida State University, where he practices group
    and family psychology as well as trains and supervises
    doctoral and post-doctoral trainees

Children
of the
Aging Self–Absorbed

A Guide to Coping with Difficult, Narcissistic Parents & Grandparents

Nina W. Brown, EdD, LPC

New Harbinger Publications, Inc.

Publisher's Note

This publication is designed to provide accurate and authoritative information in regard to the subject matter covered. It is sold with the understanding that the publisher is not engaged in rendering psychological, financial, legal, or other professional services. If expert assistance or counseling is needed, the services of a competent professional should be sought.

Distributed in Canada by Raincoast Books

Copyright © 2015 by Nina W. Brown
        New Harbinger Publications, Inc.
        5674 Shattuck Avenue
        Oakland, CA 94609
        www.newharbinger.com

Cover design by Amy Shoup
Acquired by Melissa Valentine
Edited by Brady Kahn

Library of Congress Cataloging-in-Publication Data on file

Printed in the United States of America

19   18   17

10   9   8   7   6   5   4   3   2

This book is dedicated to my family, who continue to give me encouragement, support, and, most of all, joy.

Contents

Preface

Aging is a natural part of life and brings many changes to and for each of us. Many of these changes happen gradually over time and may go unnoticed until they reach a certain point where we become aware of them and can no longer deny them. Many books and other resources are available to guide people through the aging process and to provide an understanding of age-related conditions. This book has a different focus: it guides you as the adult child of a self-absorbed parent who is aging, to help you gain a better understanding of how your parent's aging may affect his or her already self-absorbed behaviors and attitudes and to provide coping suggestions for how to succeed and thrive in spite of them.

Emphasized are your thoughts, feelings, and reactions, as these are your resources for a constructive building of your self that will withstand the negative impact of your parent's behavior and attitudes on your conscious and unconscious self-perception, self-confidence, and self-esteem. The focus will not be on the self-absorbed parent, as your parent is unlikely to change. Unfortunately, there is little or nothing that you can do to promote and encourage positive change for your parent. However, there is much you can do to promote and encourage positive change for yourself.

You may now have a family you created in addition to your family of origin and be concerned about how your self-absorbed parent can and does negatively affect your created family. You may want to protect your family from distressing behaviors and attitudes that you've encountered all your life, as you know very well how hurtful and destructive they can be. This book describes how you can prepare yourself and your family, offers possible interventions when interacting with your parent, and gives some strategies for minimizing your parent's negative impact on your family members. Finally, this book is intended to encourage and support you in your own growth and development and to guide you in finding personal solutions.

Chapters 1 and 2 describe some of the concerns and problems with aging that can increase a parent's already self-absorbed behaviors and attitudes and cover four types of self-absorbed parents. Chapters 3 and 4 focus on your reactions and thinking processes in response to a self-absorbed parent and on how to be more effective. Chapters 5 through 7 offer some suggestions for how to communicate with your parent and cope. Chapter 8 helps you manage conflict and assaultive confrontations. Chapters 9 and 10 provide you with some additional strategies for protecting yourself and your family members and loved ones. Chapter 11 summarizes how to use the strategies in this book, so that you can reduce or eliminate your self-absorbed parent's influence on you, and how to succeed and thrive in your life.

It is my hope that the material in this book will be helpful. While your parent's behaviors and attitudes were influential in your development, they do not have to continue to impact you. You can overcome the negative impact and become the person you want to be.

Acknowledgments

It is important to acknowledge the ideas, concepts, and contributions of others who helped in the development of this book. The ideas and concepts developed by mental health professionals through the years, the research on treatment strategies, and my colleagues from the Society of Group Psychology and Group Psychotherapy and the American Group Psychotherapy Association continually trigger a better understanding of difficult and narcissistic people, and I appreciate the work that they do.

No book is created in isolation. Acknowledged are the contributions by New Harbinger's Acquisitions Editor Melissa Valentine, Editorial Manager Jess Beebe, and Associate Editor Nicola Skidmore. My sincere thanks to all of you.

CHAPTER 1

Aging and the Self-Absorbed Parent

The following vignette describes a painful dilemma frequently encountered by adult children of self-absorbed parents.

DENNIS'S STORY

Dennis had been on edge for the past two weeks ever since his father, who lived in another state, announced that he and Dennis's mother were coming to visit Dennis and his family. While Dennis had told his wife about the proposed visit, they had agreed to delay telling the children—Bob, age nine, and Cybil, age seven—because neither child liked their grandfather. This dislike was so intense that the children refused to ride in the car with their grandfather unless Dennis was with them. Dennis was really dreading the visit.

Dennis found it hard to describe what his father did that caused such dislike by his family, and although he had a lifetime of experiencing his father's behavior and attitudes, he could not put words to what was so troubling about them. When he talked about his father, he could only say that his father was arrogant, gave orders, and expected prompt obedience and compliance, that he lacked empathy, and that he expected everyone to admire him.

Dennis knew that his father was beginning to show some signs of aging and wasn't pleased about it, but Dennis had hoped that aging would result in some positive changes for his father, such as becoming more aware and sensitive to the impact of what he said and did. So far, none of this had happened, and Dennis feared that his father's actions during his visit would have a devastating effect on his wife and children.

Like Dennis, if your parent is self-absorbed, you've been dealing with some negative and distressing behaviors and attitudes for probably as long as you can remember, and these behaviors and attitudes have probably only gotten worse as your parent aged. What you need are some practical strategies to use to protect yourself and your children, your spouse or partner, and others in your intimate world who have to interact with your parent.

This book focuses on how aging impacts the self-absorbed parent, how it impacts the parent's relationships with others and especially you, the adult child, and how you can productively and effectively cope. It will help you develop new ways to withstand your parent's negative assaults. It will give you some specific strategies for managing the difficult and intense feelings that can be triggered when you and your parent are in the presence of others, such as at holidays and during other celebrations. Other people will not know your parent as you do, and these strategies can help you prevent conflict, confrontation, and potential embarrassment.

As the adult child of an aging parent, you may face certain issues that cannot be adequately addressed here, and you may need to consult other books and resources to address these issues. Numerous resources are available to help you with caretaking, finding assisted living and nursing home facilities, caring for people with Alzheimer's and dementia, hospice and palliative care, legal issues such as wills and trusts, home renovations for the elderly, and other end-of-life concerns.

This book will help you attain these objectives:

- Gaining an understanding of some different aspects of aging and how these may affect your parent and you

- Learning how to decrease your self-absorbed parent's negative effects on you

- Protecting yourself, your children or grandchildren, and your spouse or partner

- Managing difficult and sometimes intense negative feelings, such as guilt and shame

- Surviving celebrations, such as parties and holidays, when your parent is present

- Learning ways to respond to your parent that are effective and appropriate for both you and your parent

- Developing a stronger and more resilient self

There are exercises in this book to help you achieve these objectives, and you are encouraged to complete these. The exercises are designed to clarify and focus your perceptions about your parent and yourself, to increase your understanding of what it means to have a self-absorbed aging parent, and to trigger some creative ideas for coping that are in accord with your personality.

SOME ASSUMPTIONS ABOUT YOU

The material in this book is based on some assumptions about you. Not all of those that are listed may be reflective of you, but many may be:

- You are an adult child who has one or more self-absorbed parents.

- You can feel ineffective much of the time in interactions with your parent.

- You have been given the responsibility for your parent's psychological and emotional well-being and, either now or in the future, are expected to assume responsibility for your parent's physical well-being.

- You never feel that you have accomplished enough for your parent; what you do never seems to be good enough.

- You experience numerous difficult situations and interactions with your self-absorbed parent.

- You are searching for ways to minimize how your parent's distressing behaviors and attitudes affect you.

- You want to intervene to protect those nearest to you, such as your children, from the negative and distressing comments, put-downs, criticisms, and the like that your parent continues to make.

Distressing feelings may arise as you read this book and do the exercises. Before diving in, it may be helpful for you to complete an exercise that's designed to help you manage distressing feelings should they arise.

Exercise 1.1:   Distract and Discover

Materials: One or more sheets of paper, a pen or pencil, and a suitable surface for writing, such as a table or a large book

Procedure:

1. Sit in silence and allow yourself to think of two or three activities that you can easily use as distractions for the moment. List these on a sheet of paper. Here are some possible examples: counting the number of items in a jar, such as jelly beans, marbles, paper clips, or buttons; organizing a drawer; rubbing a smooth stone; mindful meditation.

2. Now choose one of these activities and list the materials that you would need to have available to do it when you start to experience a distressing feeling. For example, if counting buttons in a jar is an activity that would help divert your attention, then you would need to have a jar and buttons available.

3. Obtain the materials and keep them near at hand. You may not need the activity, but it can be a comfort to know that you can get away from distressing feelings, if only for the time frame you are engaged with it.

4. Use the rest of the sheet of paper or another sheet to list any and all distractions you have used or could use. Put them into these categories:

- Activities you enjoy that are either cost-free or very cheap. Examples could be dancing around the room, singing, playing air guitar, or creating a collage from found items.

- Chores such as raking leaves, pulling weeds, or cleaning out the kitchen cabinets

- Performing acts of kindness

- Creative activities, such as knitting, art, music, sewing, cooking, woodworking, or fixing something

5. Place your lists where you can readily find them, and pledge to do something from one of these categories to distract yourself whenever you experience distressing feelings.

Doing these activities can help you manage distressing feelings not only when reading this book but also after interacting with or even thinking about your self-absorbed parent.

Let's move to examining some of the effects of aging and why these matter, especially for the relationship with your self-absorbed parent.

WHY YOUR PARENT'S AGING MATTERS

Aging is a phase of life that brings changes that are inevitable and that can be distressing, although each person will have a different set of changes and concerns. Most changes happen gradually and may not be noticed or appreciated by anyone other than the person who is experiencing them, and responses to these changes can vary from limited acceptance to complete denial. The changes that may occur as a result of aging can be categorized as physical, cognitive, relational, emotional, financial, and existential. Some examples are listed below. As you review them, you may want to reflect on the extent to which your parent is experiencing any of these changes, or other such changes as a part of aging, and on how important they are for your parent.

Physical Changes

Impact on appearance, such as wrinkles, sagging skin

Alcohol or drug dependence

Development of chronic or acute illnesses

Increased use of medications and the side effects for these

Decreased energy, vigor

Decline in sex drive, pleasure

Sensory impairment, such as for vision, hearing, or taste

Insomnia, sleep difficulties

Increasingly constant aches and pain

Cognitive Changes

Short-term and long-term memory decline

Thinking decline, or cognitive impairment

Decline in ability to acquire new knowledge

Difficulty adjusting to new ideas or changes

Relational Changes

Greater social isolation

Increasing fear of dependency on others

Divorce or increasing estrangement from spouse

Death of spouse, relatives, or friends

Emotional Changes

Awareness of lost dreams or missed opportunities

Increasing envy over others' accomplishments

Fear of becoming irrelevant, minimized, ignored, or overlooked

Depression or depressed mood

Financial Changes

Loss of income or potential loss

Concerns about protecting assets for end-of-life challenges

Increased cost of health care, such as assisted living or nursing-home care

Existential Changes

Greater focus on the meaning and purpose for life

Facing the inevitability of death

End-of-life concerns

Feelings of loneliness or alienation

As you can see, many changes may accompany the aging phase of life, and many are unpleasant to even contemplate. Aging self-absorbed parents may not react well to the changes they are experiencing, particularly since many of these changes are not under their control.

YOUR PARENT'S SELF-ABSORBED CHARACTERISTICS

You may have already identified your parent as being self-absorbed. Every self-absorbed parent is different, however, and the following scale will help you to identify how your own parent displays self-absorption. This will better enable you to focus on this book's suggestions for coping with your parent's distressing behaviors.

Exercise 1.2: Parental Self-Absorbed Behaviors and Attitudes Scale

Materials: A sheet of paper and a pen or pencil

Procedure: Find a place to work where you will not be disturbed. Use the sheet of paper to make a list of numbers from 1 to 13 for each item on the scale. Rate the extent to which your parent fits the description on each item:

1—Never or almost never displays this behavior or attitude

2—Seldom displays this behavior or attitude

3—Somewhat reflective of parent's behaviors or attitudes

4—Very reflective of parent's behaviors or attitudes

5—Extremely reflective of parent's behaviors or attitudes

1. Grandiosity

   An inflated self-perception of being superior, more capable, or more influential than others, even when there may be evidence that this is not a valid self-perception.

2. The impoverished self

   This is the other side of grandiosity, the deflated self, the inadequate self that is in danger of being abandoned or destroyed because it is fatally flawed. This state can alternate with grandiosity very quickly for your parent, which can be confusing.

3. Entitlement attitude

   People with this attitude are convinced that they deserve preferential treatment; that others should give them what they desire without any hesitation or question; and that they should not have to ask for what they need or want. They also tend to assume that rules do not apply to them.

4. Attention seeking

   This behavior is designed to draw other people's attention. Examples include sulking, talking loudly, interrupting others, telling lots of jokes, or wearing unusual attention-grabbing clothing or makeup.

5. Admiration hungry

   Those with this quality engage in behaviors designed to bring other people's attention to them. Examples include constantly fishing for compliments, being overly responsive to flattery, and seeking numerous awards or other recognitions.

6. Unique and special

   A need to be thought of as being unique and special and to have others respond as if this were a given.

7. Lack of empathy

   The most important defining characteristic for the self-absorbed is an inability to empathize with anyone. While no one will be able to be empathic with everyone all of the time, it is reasonable to expect that adults will be able to empathize with many people most of the time.

8. Exploits others

   Exploitation includes manipulating others to do things that are not in their best interests. These acts are accompanied with the perception that others deserve it, should not object, and should not expect any favors in return. Exploiters will lie, cheat, distort, and mislead to get what they want, to demonstrate their power and control, and to show up others as being inferior.

9. Shallow emotions

   Self-absorbed people have a restricted range of emotions, primarily anger and fear. They may appear to express other emotions, but they do not feel them or understand them, nor do they really understand other emotions when other people express them.

10. Inappropriate sense of humor

    Telling or laughing at jokes that demean other people or groups of people, the use of insulting and invalidating terms for groups of people, poking fun at others' disabilities or characteristics over which they have no control, or saying anything that is intended to be shaming.

11. Emptiness at the core

This can be felt as a lack of meaning and purpose in life, a sense of being adrift without an anchor or direction; alienation, isolation, and loneliness; a yearning for meaningful connections; and a dread of encountering that inner emptiness. A sense of emptiness may also be observed when someone has had many failed relationships, is unable to initiate and maintain enduring and satisfying relationships, flits from one activity or interest to another, and is generally dissatisfied.

12. Extensions of self

Self-absorbed people can have a faulty perception that others are extensions of themselves and thus are under their control. They expect others to cater to them and not to have separate lives, to understand that their purpose for living is to ensure the self-absorbed person's well-being. They also expect other people to respond to their needs, wishes, and desires without protest and without having to be told explicitly what to do or what is wanted.

13. Envy

Envy is the perception and feeling that others have something that they do not merit and that whatever it is should belong to the envious person instead. Others are thought to be less worthy, capable, or deserving than the envious person and have somehow managed to gain something that is not rightfully theirs.

Scoring

Add your ratings for items numbered 1 through 13 to derive a total score. _____

Total scores will range from 13 to 65 and can indicate the extent of your parent's self-absorption.

> 55 to 65—Your parent displays mostly self-absorbed attitudes and behaviors almost all of the time.

45 to 54—Your parent displays many self-absorbed attitudes and behaviors much of the time.

35 to 44—Your parent frequently displays some self-absorbed attitudes and behaviors.

25 to 34—Your parent sometimes displays some self-absorbed attitudes and behaviors.

13 to 24—Your parent never or almost never displays self-absorbed attitudes and behaviors.

Total scores of 35 and above indicate that the parent displays many self-absorbed behaviors and attitudes.

Next, make a list of all the behaviors and attitudes that you rated 4 or 5. These will be the categories of behaviors and attitudes that carry the most distress for you, and they can be your focus for evaluating the suggested coping strategies in coming chapters.

As you examine your parent's self-absorbed behaviors and attitudes, there are a few primary points to keep in mind:

- People who exhibit these particular troubling behaviors and attitudes are unaware that they have these attitudes or that they display these behaviors and are indifferent to the impact of these on others.

- This inability to perceive that a behavior or attitude is troubling to others means that it is futile to try to bring it to the parent's attention. In other words, do not try to make your parent see what you see, as it will not work or be constructive and it also has the potential to make the relationship or interaction worse.

- The self-absorbed person's well-being is central to him in all interactions and relationships; the self-absorbed person is constantly in a state of protecting his own interests.

- No single characteristic is reflective of self-absorption. To be categorized as self-absorbed, the person must display several characteristics and have these characteristics verified by other people who interact with this person on a regular basis.

You may find that one or both of your parents could be rated as self-absorbed. It is also possible for a parent to exhibit certain self-absorbed behaviors and attitudes but to do so less frequently or less intensely than described here. That does not mean that these behaviors or attitudes are any less troubling to you and to your relationship with that parent.

To be fair and objective, it will be helpful to identify some positive behaviors and attitudes that your parent exhibits. The positive behaviors and attitudes in the next scale can also be a guide for your self-development, as you will want to work to develop these behaviors and attitudes if you do not already have them.

HEALTHY AND CONSTRUCTIVE ADULT NARCISSISM

It can be helpful to consider narcissism as a necessary and vital component for self-concept that has to be developed to be healthy and constructive for adults. This process of development occurs along a continuum, where intense self-absorption is expected for infants and children and is expected to progress in growth toward healthy and constructive narcissism for adolescents and adults. However, the development can become mired and stuck for some adolescents and adults, where the behaviors and attitudes they display are more reflective of the earlier state expected for infants and children. For example, grandiosity is expected for children, where they consider themselves wonderful, as being able to do anything, and are intensely focused on their own wishes, needs, and demands. However, the same behaviors and attitudes for adolescents and adults are not so endearing and can be troubling for relationships. When adults remain stuck in these earlier behaviors and attitudes of self-absorption, it can be termed pathological or diagnosed as a narcissistic personality disorder.

So far, the focus has been on the negative behaviors and attitudes of adult self-absorption. Now let's move on to considering some of the attributes of healthy and constructive adult narcissism. The latter is actually an ideal state of being. That is, some adults can have many or most of the attributes of healthy and constructive narcissism, but few have all of them. These are the behaviors and attitudes that must be cultivated as a part of an individual's personal growth and development. As they develop and increase, there is an accompanying reduction of self-absorbed behaviors and attitudes.

Exercise 1.3: Parental Positive Attributes Scale

Materials: A sheet of paper and a pen or pencil for writing

Procedure: Find a place to work where you will not be disturbed. Make a list numbered 1 to 14 to correspond with each of the items on the scale. Rate the extent to which your parent's behaviors or attitudes fit the description on each item:

1—Not like parent; never or almost never does this

2—Unsure if this fits parent; seldom if ever does this

3—Somewhat like parent; can do this on occasion

4—Much like parent; frequently does this

5—Very much like parent; always or almost always does this

1. Shows empathy

   Demonstrates the capacity to enter the world of the other person, to feel what that person is experiencing without losing the sense of self as being separate and distinct, and to accurately convey those feelings in words to the other person.

2. Creative

Uses the ability to provide new and novel initiatives in everyday life, to be flexible in thought and actions, and to make constructive use of imagination.

3. Exhibits appropriate sense of humor

Is able to see the humor in life's absurdities and in events that are not harmful or shameful for others. Refuses to laugh at others' unfortunate conditions. Does not use slurs, put-downs, or sarcasm and sees no humor in differences over which others have no control, such as race and gender.

4. Wisdom

Demonstrates through words and action an ability to capitalize on life experiences and to learn from mistakes made by self or others. Understands when and how to intervene, has confidence in self and confidence in others to take care of their needs, and has developed a sense of personal meaning and purpose for life but remains open to possibilities.

5. Self-reflective

Takes time to consider personal values and priorities before taking action. Also can engage in self-examination so as to reduce self-absorbed behaviors and attitudes. Does not automatically dismiss unpleasant feedback from others but can carefully consider the worth and value of this feedback without becoming narcissistically wounded or angry.

6. Beauty, wonder, and zest

Is able to see beauty and wonder in everyday life, appreciates the various forms in which they can appear, and searches for new expressions of them.

7. Balances self-care with care for others

Accepts appropriate responsibility for caring for self and for others; nurtures and cares for children, the elderly, and those who have a temporary or lasting need for caring and nurturing. Can have others' needs as priorities, when necessary, but can also distinguish between his own needs and priorities and those of others.

8. Emotionally expressive

   Has and expresses a wide range and variety of emotions and can manage and contain intense and unpleasant emotions.

9. Recognizes separateness of self and others

   Demonstrates an appreciation for others as being worthwhile, unique, and separate from oneself and as having the capability and responsibility for caring for themselves.

10. Cultivates resiliency

    Deeply feels the impact of life's negative events, takes stock of internal resources that can be used to foster self-efficacy, and uses these resources to help overcome life's adversities.

11. Lives by a set of freely chosen values

    Does not blindly accept the values proposed by others, even those that were a part of earlier development, but instead examines these and makes a conscious choice to accept or to reject them and seek out other values that are more fulfilling. Chooses and uses values to guide moral and ethical decision making and actions.

12. Altruistic

    Can freely give to others when appropriate and does not expect reciprocity.

13. Initiates and maintains meaningful and enduring relationships

    Has long-term friends, less than three marriages that ended in divorce, and is not exploitive of relationships.

14. Has strong and resilient psychological boundaries

    Demonstrates an understanding of where self ends and others begin. Is not easily manipulated or bullied, does not engage in manipulative or bullying actions, and does not become enmeshed in or overwhelmed by others' emotions.

Scoring

Add your ratings for numbers 1 through 14 to derive a total score.

Total scores will range from 14 to 70 and can indicate the extent of your parent's positive attributes.

57 to 70—Your parent has numerous positive attributes and considerable healthy adult narcissism.

43 to 56—Your parent has many positive attributes and some healthy adult narcissism.

29 to 42—Your parent can demonstrate a few positive attributes at times.

14 to 28—Your parent has a few positive attributes but rarely demonstrates them.

Make a list of the most positive attributes, those you rated as 4 or 5, and keep the list as a reminder that your parent does have positive attributes. While the parent may have more troubling behaviors and attitudes, it is balancing to remain aware that there are also positive ones.

You can take the additional step of rating yourself on each of the positive attributes in the previous exercise. If your score is lower than you would like, doing this exercise will reveal which attributes you can work on to build your healthy adult narcissism.

HOW YOUR PARENT'S AGING IMPACTS YOU

You may be very aware of some of your immediate reactions, thoughts, and feelings, but you may not realize how your parent's aging may be impacting your thoughts and feelings about your self (the inner you), your perceptions of others and your relationships with them, and even some of your other behaviors and attitudes. The remainder of the book presents information and activities designed to promote your understanding.

Perhaps the most helpful for the immediate present and for the future are the coping strategies presented here that are designed to help reduce the negative feelings, thoughts, and behaviors that can result from interacting with your parent. For example, some of your parent's comments may produce rage, which is very uncomfortable and can be difficult to relinquish. Your parent's negative comments and your reactions can also impact your behavior, relationships, and self-perception without you being aware of how these are being influenced. The information in this book will help to increase your awareness of how your parent's behaviors and attitudes and your reactions to them impact and influence you, and will also help you to manage and contain negative emotions. Presented are some immediate coping strategies and a guide to developing longer term ones in accord with your personality.

Central to coping—and to eliminating the negative impact on you—is your self-development. This means developing your inner self to have strength and wisdom, having positive self-esteem that is neither inflated nor deflated, recognizing reasonable expectations and limitations for your responsibility for others' well-being, having an ability to express a wide range of emotions in appropriate ways, being able to develop and maintain satisfying and enduring relationships, becoming inspired and creative, and other positive outcomes. A significant part of the book will focus on positive self-development. A positive side effect of undertaking self-development is that doing so will enable you to develop long-term coping strategies that are consistent with your personality and needs.

The activities in this book are designed to do the following:

- Increase your awareness of nonconscious and unconscious thoughts, feelings, and ideas

- Teach preventive and protective actions

- Stimulate your inner self to produce positive coping strategies

- Increase your hardiness and resiliency

- Give you examples of how you can resist contributing to your own distress

- Help you develop positive responses that reduce the negative impact of your parent's behaviors and attitudes on you and on others

You are encouraged to try all of the activities, even if they do not appear to be appealing. Reaching the intended objectives is a process, and these activities are a guide or a stimulus to aid you in achieving them. At the end of this chapter, you will find some suggested activities that will anchor and protect you as you work your way through the book, and they can also be useful during and after interactions with a self-absorbed parent.

The next chapter helps identify the type of self-absorbed parent you may have: clingy, suspicious/defensive, arrogant, or belligerent. Presented also are some commonalities across the different types. Subsequent chapters focus on your typical responses and reactions, why they may not be effective, and how to develop more effective responses and reactions.

SOME SHORT-TERM SUGGESTIONS

Growing, developing, and healing are long-term processes, and there can be some setbacks along the way because of having to endure the negative effects of your self-absorbed parent. Following are some suggestions for managing your interactions and feelings until you can sort out what will work best for you in dealing with your parent:

- If you have siblings, it can be helpful to remember that they have a different relationship with your parent and may have a very different point of view from yours. Do not try to convince them of the validity of your perceptions, as this can only lead to you becoming even more frustrated and may rupture this relationship.

- Do not try to enlist your siblings' assistance with the parent. It is more likely that you will need to manage your interactions by yourself.

- Do not bring other family members, such as the other parent, into conflicts you have with the self-absorbed parent, and do not express your concerns to them. You may need to assume that they will disclose what you say to the parent, either intentionally or unintentionally, and this can make bad matters worse.

■ Monitor your disclosures to the self-absorbed parent, such as concerns and issues you are facing that involve your children or spouse. If you need to talk about these matters, find someone who is not a family member with whom you can talk about problems and who will keep this information confidential.

■ If you are not financially independent from your parent, make plans to become independent. This can help prevent you from being manipulated because you need or want financial assistance.

These are some basic suggestions that you can begin to consider implementing, as they can be very helpful in reducing some of the stress that occurs from your interactions with your self-absorbed parent. You may also find the following suggestion about journaling to be very helpful.

Keeping a Journal

Journaling has been found to be helpful in a number of ways, especially to reduce stress and anxiety. You may want to try to keep a journal of your feelings, thoughts, ideas, and other such internal activities as you read through this book and try the exercises. Your journal can then serve to document your journey to a greater understanding of your parent and of yourself—your increasing awareness of the effects of aging for your parent and for you as the adult child—and to celebrate the successes of your coping strategies.

Journals can take many forms. Two basic forms are a writing journal and a visual journal, both of which are described in the next exercise.

Exercise 1.4:   Journaling

A Writing Journal

Materials: A composition book or a commercial journal book, a pen or pencil for writing

Procedure:

1. Find a place to write where you will not be disturbed. There are no rules for writing.

2. As you complete each scale, exercise, or chapter, write about your experience in your journal. You can write about your feelings that are triggered, any awareness that emerged, or whatever comes to mind. What you write can be in complete sentences or may be phrases, words, stream of consciousness—whatever you want it to be. Grammar, punctuation, and other technical writing concerns do not apply.

3. Try to write something after each scale, exercise, or chapter, so you have a fuller account of your journey. However, it is up to you as to when and how much you write.

These are the basics for keeping a writing journal. A visual journal follows the same procedure, except that you express yourself through drawing, coloring, doodling, pasting in found objects, using cutout images to create a collage, or whatever seems to be expressive for you.

A Visual Journal

Materials: A blank book or an artist sketchbook with Bristol or water-color paper, glue, colored felt markers or pencils (or your choice of coloring medium), images cut out of magazines or other sources, found materials and objects, and stamps and ink pads

Procedure

1. Plan what you want to express, and gather the materials.

2. Begin with selecting a color for the background. Be sure to let the background dry before drawing or writing on it.

3. Draw an image or cut out an image and paste it on the page, or just use splotches of color to illustrate and express what seems to be most important for you as a result of completing a scale, exercise, or chapter. There are no rules except to visualize and create whatever meets your purpose.

4. You may want to add some words, such as some feelings or thoughts, on the illustration.

Journaling can be a mood enhancer, it can help you clarify ideas and express yourself creatively, and it can act as inspiration. One word of caution: Please be sure to keep your journal in a safe and secure place where others cannot access it. Never show your journal to your self-absorbed parent or to anyone who might disclose its existence to your parent.

SUMMARY

This chapter set the stage for what will follow in the book. So far, you may better understand how your parent's self-absorption is displayed in behaviors and attitudes as well as how and why your parent's aging is significant for both of you and for your relationship. Some new ways to cope with your parent's troubling self-absorption have also been presented. In addition, it is hoped that this book will guide you in your self-development and show you how you can succeed and thrive in spite of your self-absorbed parent.

CHAPTER 2

Types of Self-Absorbed Parents

This chapter begins with exploring the impact of your aging self-absorbed parent on you and then presents information about some types of parental self-absorption. Becoming more aware of the impact on you and the behaviors and attitudes for the different types of parent can be helpful by suggesting coping strategies that fit your self-absorbed parent's troubling behaviors and distressing attitudes that have negative impacts on you. Presented also are the commonly held behaviors and attitudes across types. You may find that your parent's behaviors and attitudes have become more intense as your parent ages. For example, your parent may have exhibited a modest entitlement attitude when you and your parent were younger, but your parent now seems to have an extreme entitlement attitude. This increased intensity is something you may want to pay attention to as you work through identifying your parental type. It is also possible, though not likely, that some of your parent's troubling behaviors or distressing attitudes have decreased in number and in intensity. For example, your parent may appear to be more empathic, but it is more likely that she has become even less empathic with age and is even more focused on her personal concerns, such as health.

YOUR PARENT'S IMPACT ON YOU

Let's explore some possible impacts of your parent's behaviors and attitudes on you. These impacts can best be understood by your reactions and the negative feelings that emerge in interactions with your parent or when you think about your parent. Following is a process for letting go of negative feelings. The first step is to identify some possible reactions you may have after interacting with your self-absorbed parent.

Exercise 2.1: Feelings Experienced When Interacting with My Parent

Materials: A sheet of paper and a pen or pencil

Procedure: Find a place to work where you will not be disturbed. Use the sheet of paper to make a list of numbers from 1 to 11 for each item on the scale. Think about some recent interactions with your parent and rate the extent to which you experienced these reactions:

  1—Never or almost never

  2—Sometimes

  3—Often

  4—Very often

  5—Always or almost always

My Reactions

1. Guilt (for not meeting expectations)

2. Shame (for not being good enough)

3. Resentment (feeling you are unfairly treated)

4. Frustration

5. Despair

6. Hopelessness

7. Dread or apprehension (of having to interact with your parent)

8. Self-doubt

9. Anger

10. Fear

11. Sadness

Scoring

Add your ratings for numbers 1 to 11 to derive a total score.

Total scores will range from 11 to 55:

46 to 55—You have numerous intensely negative feelings.

36 to 45—You have many negative feelings, some of which are intense.

26 to 35—You have some negative feelings but only a few that are intense.

Below 25—You have few negative feelings, most of which are not intense.

Scores of 36 and above can indicate that you have many negative feelings that may also be lingering and difficult to overcome.

Although feelings will be discussed in more detail later in the book, it can be helpful now for you to understand that these negative feelings can be triggered by your internal feelings about your self but also can be caught from your parent. The latter state works this way. Your parent has a feeling such as fear, does not want to experience that feeling, and gets rid of it by unconsciously projecting it onto you. You catch the projection and unconsciously identify with it, then make it your own feeling and begin to act on it. The parent has gotten rid of the distressing feeling, but you now have it and may find it difficult to discard or to not act upon. This unconscious process is called *projective identification*.

These triggered feelings, whether they come from within you or are projected onto you, can impact you in many ways, especially the feelings you have about your self. The impact can lower your self-esteem, self-confidence, self-efficacy, and, in some cases, your self-control. Coping strategies are discussed in later chapters, but here is a strategy you could try at this point.

Exercise 2.2:   Let Go of Negative Feelings

Materials: A small paper box and five to eleven different colored strips of paper (such as red, blue, purple, green, yellow, and so on)

Procedure

1. Review exercise 2.1. Put a check mark by any feelings that may have become worse or have intensified with the parent's aging.

2. Select a different colored strip of paper for each feeling that you rated 4 or 5, as well as those you identified as having become more intense over time, and write that feeling on the strip. For example, if anger was rated 4 or 5 or it has become more intense, you could select a red strip and write "anger" on it.

3. Place each strip in the small box as soon as you finish writing on it, and repeat to yourself, *I'm letting go of this.*

4. Once all of the negative feelings are written on the strips, discard the box by putting it in the trash, burning it, or throwing it away, or by another method that is environmentally appropriate.

It may be unrealistic to expect that you can get rid of these negative feelings as easily as just discarding a box. What can happen, however, is that you will let go for now or the feeling will be decreased. For example, you may feel less frustrated whereas in the past you would continue to be very frustrated for a longer period of time.

Future exercises will help you continue to work with these feelings so that you can better contain and manage them. But now let's move on to describing the four types of self-absorbed parents, and see if you can identify which type description best fits your parent. As you read and complete the exercises, try to perceive your parent's behaviors and attitudes as they are displayed currently.

FOUR SELF-ABSORBED PARENT TYPES

There are four types of self-absorbed parents presented here: clingy, suspicious/defensive, arrogant, and belligerent. *Clingy* types expect you to take care of them in almost every aspect of their life, and they primarily exhibit the impoverished self. But do not be misled by this, as the grandiose self is still present and exerting its influence in hidden ways. Since these parents consider you to be an extension of themselves and under their control, this unrealistic expectation is a never-ending one for you and may even control your life. *Suspicious/defensive* types are most likely deeply disappointed in their self and, by extension of that self, are also deeply disappointed in others, especially their children. This type always, or almost always, expects the worst, looks for the worst, and seems to gain some satisfaction when the anticipated worst thing happens. *Arrogant* types exhibit considerable grandiosity, manage to suppress the impoverished self from being seen by others, and sometimes can hide this impoverished self from their own awareness. Many of the arrogant type's behaviors and attitudes are exhibited in the effort to prevent the unsatisfactory impoverished self from being seen or known either oneself or by others. *Belligerent* types can be very unpleasant to be around, and their most distressing behaviors and attitudes can worsen as they age. They can appear to others as having considerable smoldering rage, as having hair-trigger tempers, and as being very explosive, even over matters of little or no consequence.

Each of these self-absorbed types has one or more underlying messages and goals:

Type	Messages	Goals
Clingy	*I'm helpless.*	To have others take care of them
Suspicious/ defensive	*Everyone is out to hurt me.*	Protection of the self from perceived danger
Arrogant	*You are inferior to me. I'm superior in every way.*	Keep personal inadequacies, imperfections, and the like out of conscious awareness

Belligerent	*Everyone is dangerous.*	Revenge for real or imagined psychological injuries

In the next series of exercises, you will examine the degree to which your parent may fall into one or more of the self-absorbed types.

Exercise 2.3: The Clingy Type

Materials: A sheet of paper and a pen or pencil

Procedure: Find a place to work where you will not be disturbed. Use the sheet of paper to make a list of numbers from 1 to 10 for each item on the scale. Rate the extent to which your parent fits the description on each item for the clingy type:

1—Never or almost never

2—Sometimes, rarely

3—Frequently

4—Very often

5—Always or almost always

1. Seeks or seems to seek sympathy from you and others

2. Is demanding of your time and efforts on her behalf

3. Focuses on what she does not have, is missing, or is wanted

4. Wants constant attention

5. Points out how she is suffering, seeks pity

6. Smothers you with attention, is intrusive, and the like

7. Is in the child role with you in the adult role

8. Cries easily and often

9. Expects you and others to meet her needs at the expense of your own or others' needs

10. Carps, complains, whines

Scoring

Add your ratings for numbers 1 through 10 to derive a total score.

Total scores can range from 10 to 50:

42 to 50—Extremely clingy

34 to 41—Very clingy

22 to 33—Somewhat clingy

10 to 21—Exhibits some clingy behaviors or attitudes

Scores from 34 to 50 indicate that your parent displays a significant number of clingy behaviors and attitudes. Having experienced these from birth, you may not realize the impact that these are having on you and on your other relationships. Your parent uses her need for attention and so on to keep you close and attentive so as to meet her every need, wish, and desire.

Exercise 2.4: The Suspicious/ Defensive Parent Type

Materials: A sheet of paper and a pen or pencil

Procedure: Use the sheet of paper to make a list of numbers from 1 to 10 for each item on the scale. Rate the extent to which your parent fits the description on each item for the suspicious/defensive type:

1—Never or almost never

2—Sometimes, rarely

3—Frequently

4—Very often

5—Always or almost always

1. Makes comments that suggest that she is suspicious of your motives or the motives of others

2. Assumes the most negative perception of whatever you say or do

3. Seems to feel that you are deliberately neglecting her

4. Is overly sensitive to any hint of perceived criticism

5. Expects you and others to be perfect

6. Is rigid and unbending

7. Tends to be very concrete and detailed, asks numerous questions

8. Is calculating and manipulative

9. Keeps others at a distance

10. Easily takes offense

Scoring

Add the ratings for numbers 1 through 10 to derive a total score.

_____

Total scores can range from 10 to 50:

42 to 50—Exhibits numerous and intense suspicious or defensive behaviors and attitudes

34 to 41—Exhibits many suspicious or defensive behaviors and attitudes, some of which may be intense

21 to 33—Exhibits some suspicious or defensive behaviors and attitudes sometimes, but they are not usually intense

10 to 20—May exhibit one or more suspicious or defensive attitudes and behaviors at times, but they are few and not intense

Total scores ranging from 34 to 50 suggest that your parent exhibits numerous suspicious and defensive behaviors and attitudes. You may find that you are constantly on edge and apprehensive because you never know when or how your parent will become irritated or explode. It's as if you were always on the hot seat having to answer numerous questions and uncertain of the parent's responses.

Exercise 2.5:   The Arrogant Parent

Materials: A sheet of paper and a pen or pencil

Procedure: Use the sheet of paper to make a list of numbers from 1 to 12 for each item on the scale. Rate the extent to which your parent fits the description on each item for the arrogant type:

1—Never or almost never

2—Sometimes, rarely

3—Frequently

4—Very often

5—Always or almost always

1. Displays a superior attitude

2. Boasts and brags about personal possessions, accomplishments, and the like

3. Takes unearned credit for others' achievements

4. Fails to assume responsibility for mistakes

5. Exhibits an entitlement attitude

6. Is contemptuous of you or others

7. Is quick to point out others' deficiencies and mistakes

8. Feels that you owe her

9. Assumes she is right and should always receive deference

10. Feels that she has the right to take advantage of others

11. Gives orders and expects prompt compliance

12. Is sarcastic

Scoring

Add the ratings for numbers 1 through 12 to derive a total score.

Total scores can range from 12 to 60.

51 to 60—Exhibits considerable arrogant behaviors and attitudes almost all of the time

41 to 50—Frequently exhibits many arrogant attitudes and behaviors

31 to 40—Will sometimes display some arrogant attitudes and behaviors

21 to 30—Infrequently displays arrogant attitudes and behaviors

20 and below—Almost never displays any arrogant attitudes or behaviors

Total scores from 41 to 60 indicate that the parent displays numerous arrogant behaviors and does so frequently or almost all of the time. You and others are expected to show deference, to provide attention and admiration, and to accept the parent's superiority in every way. What can be difficult to accept is the contempt the parent can show at any time toward you and others.

Exercise 2.6:   The Belligerent Parent

Materials: A sheet of paper and a pen or pencil

Procedure: Use the sheet of paper to make a list of numbers from 1 to 10 for each item on the scale. Rate the extent to which your parent fits the description on each item for the belligerent type:

1—Never or almost never

2—Sometimes, rarely

3—Frequently

4—Very often

5—Always or almost always

1. Seems angry

2. Is combative even about trivial matters

3. Criticizes and blames you and others for her personal discomfort

4. Is quick to take offense at perceived insults, slights, and the like

5. Carries grudges

6. Talks loudly and fast

7. Interrupts others, talks over others

8. Promotes discord and conflict among others

9. Can be easily angered

10. Teases and taunts others until they become distressed

Scoring

Add the ratings for numbers 1 through 10 to derive a total score.

Total scores can range from 10 to 50.

42 to 50—Displays all or almost all belligerent behaviors and attitudes almost always

34 to 41—Frequently displays many belligerent behaviors and attitudes

22 to 33—Sometimes displays some belligerent attitudes and behaviors

21 and below—Infrequently or almost never displays belligerent behaviors and attitudes

Scores ranging from 34 to 50 indicate that your parent displays a considerable number of belligerent behaviors and attitudes and does so frequently or almost all of the time. You've been exposed to these behaviors and attitudes since birth and may have found ways to cope with these. However, even if you are coping, they can still have a negative impact on you and especially on others who may have to interact with your parent on a regular basis.

Your parent's behaviors and attitudes may clearly fall into one category, but it is possible that more than one category can apply. In the latter event, use the highest total score to keep in mind and work with first as you read through the book, and then work with the other categories in the same way.

Commonly Held Attributes

All or almost all self-absorbed parents, regardless of type, will usually have certain attributes to some extent. Their attempts to cope with their aging or to deny its influences can intensify the negative impact of these attributes: envy, lack of empathy, inner emptiness, shallow emotions, and projections.

ENVY

As the self-absorbed parent's life declines and changes in almost every aspect, envy can emerge even more. This can be especially troubling for the adult child or children when they are successful or, in some cases, exceed the success of the parent. Instead of being proud and admiring, the parent resents the child's success and may say or do things that suggest that the child is unworthy or did not earn the success, which can be very hurtful.

LACK OF EMPATHY

A lack of empathy becomes even more pronounced with age. Self-absorbed parents may ignore the adult child's distress, change the topic when uncomfortable or negative feelings are expressed, discount or minimize the impact of an emotion on the adult child, and seek to invalidate the child's feelings. Other signs of a lack of empathy are abrupt changes of topic if something important to the adult child is being discussed, blaming or critical comments, encouraging self-doubt in the adult child, and making demeaning, devaluing comments about the child.

INNER EMPTINESS

The emptiness at the core of the essential self can be especially frightening for a self-absorbed parent, and because aging allows existential concerns, such as the inevitability of death, to emerge, this emptiness can become harder to deny or repress. The parent may expend considerable effort to ensure that her emptiness is not experienced on a conscious level, but it's also reasonable to expect that this emptiness exerts an influence even when it is on the unconscious level.

If emptiness is experienced, an aging parent can become even more consumed with her concerns to the detriment of anyone else's concerns. She can become totally focused on herself and have no patience or understanding that others too will have personal concerns that are focused elsewhere. She can feel that she is the center of everyone's universe and intends to remain so.

SHALLOW EMOTIONS

Your self-absorbed parent probably exhibited shallow emotions your entire life. Her self-absorption may allow her to experience and express only fear, guilt, shame, and anger. Any expressions of happiness, appreciation, love, and other positive emotions are likely to be words only, without the underlying feelings. The difference as the parent ages is that she will tend to express her negative feelings more often, and these feelings will appear to be more intense when they are expressed. It can be difficult to try to interact with someone who can express only uncomfortable and distressing feelings.

PROJECTIONS

Self-absorbed people tend to be strong emotional senders. As described earlier, the catching of usually negative feelings can be especially troubling for children who are open to projections of the parent's distressing feelings; even when these children become adults, they can find the parent's projections difficult to relinquish. Since the self-absorbed parent seems to have only distressing feelings, these are the ones that the parent wants to get rid of, and so the parent projects these feelings onto others. In some cases, adult children may have learned how to insulate themselves from taking in the projected feelings of the parent, but many adult children either have not learned that they need to insulate themselves or lack the means to do so. If you fall into either of these latter categories, or you just want a refresher on how to prevent catching the parent's feelings, complete the following exercise.

Exercise 2.7:   Emotional Insulation

Materials: One or more sheets of paper for drawing and a set of crayons, felt markers, colored pencils

Procedure:

1. Find a place to work where you will not be disturbed and that also has a suitable surface for drawing available.

2. Sit in silence and allow a picture of an event where your self-absorbed parent disapproved of you to emerge. Try to use a relatively benign event that has some negative connotations for you, but do not use an event that could cause you to become very distressed as the image emerges.

3. Now try to visualize something between you and the parent during the event, something that insulates you from the disapproval or other negative emotions the parent may have. You could visualize fiberglass insulation, a bale of straw, heavy shatterproof glass, or anything that feels like it could be insulating.

4. Once you have visualized the insulation, use the materials to draw a picture or image of the insulation between you and your parent.

5. Finally, write a few words that describe your insulation, such as "heavy," "protective," "strong," and so on.

You now have an image of your insulation and the words you used to describe it, which you can use whenever you need to. It will be most helpful if you can visualize the insulation before interacting with your parent, but it can still work if you use it at any time during an interaction.

What follows is a more complete description of the four types of self-absorbed parents. As you read these descriptions, try to think of what you can do to better cope with the feelings that the parent arouses in you.

The Clingy Type

Clingy self-absorbed parents are likely to have excessive needs like the following:

- Constantly seeking attention

- Hungry for admiration

- An attitude that they be considered as unique and special

- Feeling entitled

- Being willing to exploit others

- Trying to fill an inner emptiness

These parents can be needy for attention, admiration for how much they have to endure, and recognition of their uniqueness and special-ness; for you and others to have their desires and wishes as priorities; and for you and others to act so that their core emptiness will not be experienced. As these parents age, their needs can become overwhelming for them, which leads to their being extremely demanding of your and others' time, efforts, and appreciation. Aging only increases their self-absorbed behaviors, attitudes, wishes, needs, and desires, as real maladies can emerge that intensify their demands on others, but there is nothing you or others can do that is sufficient.

A clingy type of parent's neediness can be wearing, as it is a constant and cannot be fulfilled. No matter how much the adult child does, it is never enough. You may find it impossible to get away from the constant carping, complaining, moaning, and whining about how bad off they are and how much adversity they have to endure. They seem to always find a way to let you know how much they are suffering and that you are supposed to take better care of them so that they do not have to suffer in any way. These clingy types cannot perceive anyone as not being focused on them, and they can be especially demanding of their adult children.

What can be very frustrating for you as the adult child is that your clingy parent expects you not only to take care of her, to meet excessive expectations and demands and the like, but to do all of this without having to be told to do so. You are expected to intuitively know what the parent wants, needs, or desires without the parent having to say a word, and your parent can become deeply disappointed because you are unable to complete this impossible task all of the time. Complicating matters can be the parent's words:

- "I don't want to be a bother."

- "Don't worry about me, I'll manage."

- "I don't really need or expect you to do anything."

- "I really don't want to be a burden to you."

The real meaning can be the opposite of the words and can arouse your guilt and shame so that you find that you do try harder to meet unspoken needs and are continually frustrated. This type of self-absorbed parent can never be completely satisfied, be pleased at efforts you and others make to meet unspoken or even spoken demands, or experience having enough.

If you have tried any of the following, you probably found that it was not successful:

- Trying to give the parent what she wanted or demanded

- Asserting your separateness and independence from the parent

- Attempting to set reasonable boundaries for demands, use of your time, and so on

- Giving the parent more of your time and attention than is reasonable or that you want to give

- Making your parent aware of your responsibilities at work and for your family, in the hope that she would understand and reduce some expectations and demands

No matter what you do or try, the clingy self-absorbed parent's demands and expectations are never ending.

The Suspicious/Defensive Type

This type of parent cannot trust anyone, including you, although there may be no rational reason for this mistrust. The parent is always in a defensive position, eternally vigilant for any hint of betrayal or attack on her. You may also experience the expectation that you can read her mind and anticipate what she means, wants, or needs, and that you will provide these without her having to ask or verbalize anything. The parent asks numerous questions about almost everything and may do so in a manner that is more like an interrogation than a show of interest. Worse can be when she expects you to anticipate what she wants to know and to provide that information on your own. If you fail to do so, she can then become upset or enraged, which only leads to an increased suspicion that you are deliberately trying to mislead her.

This type of parent can only feel safe when everything is known, but since that is impossible, the parent remains suspicious and defensive, always fearing the worst will happen and that she will be hurt or will suffer negative consequences. The need to control everything intensifies with age, as the parent's ability to understand and act declines. Her awareness of the decreasing ability to protect herself arouses even more fears, which can lead to increasing demands on the adult child to provide the sought-after protection. However, no amount of anticipation of the parent's needs, providing of details, or answering questions will be enough. The search for safety and trust is constant, as the suspicious/defensive parent may have encountered past situations where the suspiciousness was reinforced by others' actions, such as a friend's betrayal.

You may have tried some or many of the following strategies without success:

- Trying to anticipate what the parent wanted to know and providing details, only to face another barrage of questions

- Asking the parent to trust you

- Restricting what you tell your parent about your life

- Waiting to tell your parent about something after it is over, in hopes that this would reduce the number of questions

- Confronting the parent with the parent's need for control

You may wonder why your parent seems to need to know everything about you: your thoughts, feelings, and ideas, as well as your actions, anticipations, and dreams. This need to know flows from the self-absorbed perspective that you are not a separate and distinct person apart from your parent, that you are an extension of the parent and, hence, under the parent's control. This self-absorbed perspective fuels the need to know everything about you so that the parent can feel in control and safe. Suspicious/defensive parents may not be aware that they have this perspective, and it is not helpful to try to make them aware of it.

The Arrogant Type

Arrogant self-absorbed parents can exhibit many infuriating characteristics such as the following:

- Never admitting to being wrong; having to always be right

- Never accepting responsibility for errors or mistakes

- Blaming and criticizing others

- Holding an attitude of superiority

- Being quick to point out how others are inferior

- Bragging and boasting, including when the accomplishment or characteristic belongs to the child

- Taking unearned credit for others' achievements and accomplishments

- Showing contempt for others

- Seeking status

- Exploiting others for personal benefit

- Expecting favors from others without any reciprocity

- Giving orders and expecting prompt obedience

The grandiose inflated self is dominant for the arrogant parent almost all or all of the time in an effort to deny, suppress, or repress the impoverished self. However, the impoverished self coexists with the inflated self and can show up at unexpected times. This is illustrated in the following example:

You are having a verbal interaction with your parent where she is blaming or criticizing you or someone else (the inflated self as being superior). You feel that the blame or criticism is unfair, so you protest or say something that would suggest that the parent is wrong or mistaken. The parent then responds with a tirade about how she tries so hard to be fair, only to face unfair accusations such as the one you just made (the impoverished self shows up). The flip-flop from grandiose to impoverished self is so rapid and unexpected that you may be unprepared to respond to the impoverished self, and you are left wondering what happened in the interaction and possibly having other distressing feelings.

You may have tried some of the following without success:

- Presenting another possibility when the parent complains about someone's actions as being unfair, suggesting that the parent could consider another possibility, and the like

- Praising and flattering the parent although you are not sincere

- Challenging the parent's inflated self-perceptions

- Recounting the achievements and accomplishments of someone else

- Trying to please the parent

Arrogant self-absorbed parents have to be dominant and perceived as superior, and can never or seldom be successfully challenged. They are responsive only to someone perceived as having higher status, and a child, even an adult child who is very successful, is never perceived as having higher status. Thus, these parents are not responsive to their child and are never likely to be responsive.

The Belligerent Type

The belligerent type of self-absorbed parent can arouse considerable fear because she seems to be hostile, is easily angered, and continually lashes out at others. Nothing seems to be done right or to her satisfaction. This type of parent derives no pleasure unless everything is perfect, according to her standards, and nothing ever meets this impossible goal. She can also carry grudges against those who hurt her. Even when this type of self-absorbed parent does not openly express anger, her facial expressions and other nonverbal gestures seem to convey angry feelings. When the worries and concerns that come with aging are added to this already existing mind-set and self-absorption, the belligerent type of parent may become even more difficult to tolerate.

Your parent may exhibit these behaviors and attitudes:

- Being easily angered or offended

- Minimally accepting or not accepting your apologies or explanations so that you continue to hear about the offense many times in the future

- Never forgetting a perceived slight, invalidation, or insult

- Usually going on the offensive, even when there appears to be no reason to do so

- Seeming to resent people who appear happier than the parent

- Feeling that she never receives the appreciation or recognition that is merited

- Always or almost always appearing to be tense

- Conveying an attitude that you owe her something and you are not meeting your obligations

Belligerent types have encountered many psychological injuries throughout their lives that have not been addressed or healed. These injuries accumulate and build on each other, producing deep psychological wounding. Because this wounding is so deep and not understood by either themselves or by others, belligerent types are put in the position where they perceive that the only protection from additional wounding is to attack first, keep others at a distance, set impossible standards, and keep others off-balance, not knowing what behavior or attitude to expect from them. These self-absorbed parents expect attacks from everyone, are constantly on guard, and strongly broadcast their discomfort.

You may have tried any of the following without success:

- Giving your parent numerous apologies, even when you don't understand what you are apologizing for or do not want to extend an apology

- Doing or saying something in an effort to please your parent, only to always find that the parent cannot be pleased

- Trying to explore with your parent the source of her anger and hostility

- Suggesting that it is time to relinquish a long-standing grudge

- Attempting to deflect or distract your parent

- Focusing on positive and happier topics

These and other such responses are not likely to work, as the parent's essential self has been hurt and did not heal. Further, because of the self-absorption, the parent may have few or no inner resources to help promote healing, may not understand or know how or when the initial wounding occurred, and perceives that the only way to prevent further hurt is to stay constantly alert and to go on the offensive at the slightest hint of potential wounding.

Your Responses

Each of the previous descriptions of self-absorbed types included a list of responses that you may have tried without success. If that's the case, you may want to charge yourself to not use those responses. They did not work with your parent in the past, they are not working now, and most likely they will not work in the future. You may want to keep the other unsuccessful responses in mind—even if you have never used them—and remember not to try these responses either, as they too are unlikely to be successful.

SUMMARY

Self-absorbed parents display many similar behaviors and attitudes, but they can differ in intensity and frequency for each parent. The self-absorbed parent types described in this chapter were intended to help you identify your parent's behaviors and attitudes, both to help you better understand your parent's goals for her behaviors and attitudes and to lessen the impact of these behaviors and attitudes on you. Awareness and understanding are the first steps you can take toward coping and thriving. The next chapter continues to build on your awareness and understanding so that you can assess the impact of your parent on you and grow in understanding of why your reactions can be ineffective; it will also suggest strategies for how to make your reactions more effective.

CHAPTER 3

Why You React as You Do

Chapters 1 and 2 described the challenges that come with aging, the difference between destructive narcissism and healthy narcissism, and the behaviors and attitudes associated with four types of self-absorbed parents. This chapter focuses on helping you identify your pattern of reactions to your self-absorbed parent. Understanding your pattern of reactions can give you a rationale for why many of your characteristic feelings and actions may be below your level of consciousness and embedded in your need to protect yourself from your parent's negative effects on you. You may also gain an understanding of why and how some of what you are doing is ineffective with your parent and perhaps in other relationships, as a first step toward becoming more effective, and have your creative thoughts triggered about how you can be more effective with your particular self-absorbed parent.

UNDERSTANDING YOUR REACTIONS

Following are some negative emotions that you may experience when interacting with your self-absorbed parent, in anticipation of an interaction with him, or even when thinking about that parent. You may even have some form of these feelings, but with less intensity, as you read this book. This discussion focuses on your feelings, not those of your parent. You can work to moderate and change your feelings, prevent them from being triggered by your parent, and learn to react in more healthy and effective ways. The negative emotions that are most common are anger, narcissistic rage, displaced anger, guilt, shame, and fear.

Anger

Think of anger as being on levels ranging from irritation, at the low or mild end, to rage at the top end. Anger falls closer to rage than to irritation on the continuum. Irritation can be easier to manage and to relinquish. There can be some bodily tension and other uncomfortable sensations, but you can still think and reason almost as you usually do when you are not irritated. Anger is the body's reaction to a perceived threat or danger, where the body prepares to fight or to flee so as to prevent the self from being destroyed. While anger manifests itself differently among individuals, many will experience considerable bodily tension. You may feel hot or flushed; your thoughts can be racing and be unreasonable or not wholly rational. You may not feel in control of yourself or of the situation. Most people can remain in control when they are angry but are very uncomfortable.

Narcissistic Rage

One of the emotions you may experience in interactions with your self-absorbed parent is narcissistic rage. This feeling is produced when the self feels in danger, and it is accompanied with feelings of helplessness to prevent the destruction of your essential self, the fear that the self will be destroyed, and a desire to do away with the instigator of these feelings about yourself. Narcissistic rage can be intense because the self seems to be in danger, and you perceive that you do not have the resources to prevent its destruction, along with also having an intense desire to destroy the offending person. You are strongly cautioned to never act on your narcissistic rage.

Displaced Anger

This is just what it sounds like: anger at one thing, situation, or person gets placed on or acted out upon something or someone else. You may even displace your anger onto yourself. An example would be when your self-absorbed parent does or says something that produces anger for you. For whatever reason, you do not allow yourself to become angry with the parent, but rather you displace that anger onto yourself and become angry with yourself. This can be what happens in other situations and relationships: you are angry with one person or situation, you do not want to be angry with that person or situation, and so you displace that anger onto someone or something else. Another example would be becoming angry at a coworker or boss and displacing it onto your spouse or friend. It could be helpful for you to become aware of when you are displacing anger, especially for your important relationships, as misdirected anger can harm these relationships.

Guilt

It would not be unusual for you to feel guilty much of the time when you are around your self-absorbed parent and even when you are apart from him. Guilt results when you perceive that you are not acting in accord with your values, such as when you have a value to care for the parent but you are resistant to doing something that the parent wants or needs. This can be one reason for having a clear idea of what your values are—for you to have examined and then freely chosen them, not have them imposed on you by others—and to do your best to act in accord with your values.

When you feel guilty, you want to do something to stop feeling this way. This is when you may need to be careful not to act on what someone else, such as your parent, wants you to do. You could use this opportunity to examine which of your values is leading to feelings of guilt. Ask yourself, *What value did I not meet? Where did I get this value from? Did I choose it, or did I unconsciously assume it?* Then you could examine the value to determine if you still want to keep and act on it or to let it go because it does not seem reasonable to you. For example, you could determine that the guilt feeling comes from an unconscious assumption and an unexamined value that you must do what the parent wants, whatever the cost to you. Once you examine the assumption underlying a value that you did not choose but unconsciously assumed, you may decide that it is not reasonable for you to do what the parent wants all of the time, that you will do what the parent wants some of the time, and that you will set a limit for what is reasonable for you to do. That choice may lead to feeling less guilty or feeling no guilt at all when you do not do everything the parent wants.

Shame

Shame is experienced when you think you aren't good enough, that you are fatally flawed, and that you are in danger of being destroyed for your inadequacies. Embarrassment is a mild form of shame and is generally experienced when others can observe your errors, mistakes, missteps, or other inadequacies. Deeper is the shame that you experience for doing and saying things that reveal flaws that you perceive as never being able to fix or overcome because you will never be good enough. Shame is easily triggered by a self-absorbed parent, as it is almost impossible to be good enough for that parent all of the time or to meet his demands.

There are many ways that people consciously and unconsciously act to prevent feeling shamed: never admitting mistakes, always having someone else to blame, pointing out others' inadequacies as distractions from their own, and using rationalizations. Some will adopt a superior attitude, continually engage in put-downs or criticisms of others (and feel entitled to do so), tell lies or make misleading statements, refuse to accept responsibility when things go wrong or they make mistakes, and exhibit other such attitudes and behaviors.

Fear

Fear can range from apprehension at the mildest to panic at the most intense. Fear at any level is a reaction to a perception that the self is in danger and will be hurt or destroyed if defensive measures are not taken. Fear produces many physical reactions: accelerated heart rate, racing thoughts, sweating, feeling very hot or very cold, tense muscles, a dry mouth, and other sensations. The body prepares for fight or flight. It may also be difficult to think logically and rationally when fearful. Reactions vary from paralysis to aggression, with many stops in between these two states.

Interactions with the self-absorbed parent can produce a range of fear reactions. You can experience apprehension, dread, fear, or even terror at just the thought of having to be in the presence of that parent. Your essential self appears to always be either under assault from that parent or under the threat of assault from that parent. Your essential self does not know how to prevent these assaults, to cope with them when they happen, or to be able to assess the severity of the threat. It is prevention and assessment of the threat that you will be working with as you progress through this book.

MODERATING YOUR FEELINGS

The feelings described here are all intense and very uncomfortable. A number of people lack awareness of the milder forms of anger, guilt, shame, and fear, and you may be among them. If you can become aware of milder forms of these feelings, such as becoming aware of when you feel apprehensive or irritated, it will allow you to take appropriate actions to prevent them from escalating. The next exercise can guide you to a better understanding of the various levels of these intense emotions.

Exercise 3.1:   Mild to Strong Feelings

Materials: A set of crayons or felt markers that has five to six shades of four different colors—for example, six shades of green, blue, red, and orange—four sheets of paper, and a pen or pencil for writing

Procedure:

1. Find a place to work where you will not be disturbed and that has a suitable writing surface.

2. Write "anger" at the top of one page, "fear" at the top of the next page, "shame" at the top of the third page, and "guilt" at the top of the fourth page.

3. Take the page labeled "anger." Choose a color for anger, select a different shade for each level of this feeling, and draw a symbol using that shade that illustrates the feeling for you, in this order, from mild to intense: irritation, displeasure, exasperation, anger, fury, rage.

4. Complete the procedure for step 3 for the feeling of fear, in this order, from mild to intense: apprehension, alarm, dread, fear, terror, panic.

5. Complete the procedure for step 3 for the feeling of shame, in this order, from mild to intense: bashful (shy), embarrassed, disgraceful, not good enough, shameful.

6. Complete the procedure for step 3 for the feeling of guilt, in this order, from mild to intense: blameful, irresponsible, faulty, remorseful, guilty, regretful.

7. Review your colors and symbols. Determine if you are able to be aware of when you feel the milder versions of each feeling or if you are only aware of feeling the intense versions.

You may want to reread the descriptions of each feeling that preceded the exercise. As you read about each feeling, try to think of how you might become more aware of the milder versions and what you can do to keep the feeling from intensifying.

Learning how to recognize when you have milder feelings can help you in interactions with your self-absorbed parent, who may easily trigger the more intense emotions, as you can take steps to prevent the intensity from escalating.

OBSERVING REACTION PATTERNS

There are three major categories of reactions: joining, fight, and flight; and all of these are characteristic patterns that usually begin in childhood and are unconsciously used. What can be most troubling for you is that your characteristic reaction pattern can continue into adulthood, where your responses to your parent are also the ones that you use in other relationships. Your adult relationships can be negatively affected because you are likely to continue to react to other people as you did with your self-absorbed parent.

Joining behaviors are those used to keep the parent happy or pleased, even at the cost of yourself. *Fight behaviors* are used to protect the self from the parent's demands and criticisms, as you erect unconscious barriers and go on the offensive to prevent attacks and their wounding. *Flight behaviors* are also used as a defense to prevent wounding and are designed to remove yourself from the battleground. The next exercise may help you understand what your reactions to your self-absorbed parent tend to be and how these reactions also may be unconsciously used with other people.

Exercise 3.2: My Characteristic Reaction Pattern

Materials: A sheet of paper and a pen or pencil

Procedure: Find a place to work where you will not be disturbed. Use the sheet of paper to make three lists of numbers from 1 to 10 for the items on the joining, fight, and flight scales that follow. Write "Joining" at the top of the first list, "Fight" at the top of the second list, and "Flight" at the top of the third list. Please rate the extent to which you do each of the following using these ratings:

1—Not like me; never or almost never do this

2—Unlike me most of the time; seldom do this

3—Like me; sometimes do this

4—Much like me; frequently do this

5—Very much like me; always or almost always do this

Joining Scale

I…

1. Adopt my parent's perspective

2. Try hard to please the parent

3. Defend the parent when he is criticized

4. Give my parent's needs priority over my needs

5. Use soothing strategies to prevent discord

6. Am easily persuaded by others to do what they want me to do

7. Find it difficult or impossible to say no and to stick to that decision

8. Give up my needs for my parent's needs

9. Can easily catch others' feelings

10. Have feelings of guilt, shame, or inadequacy that are easily triggered

Add the joining reaction ratings to derive a total score. _____

Fight Scale

I...

1. Engage in unnecessary disagreements with my parent

2. Am indifferent or try to be indifferent to my parent's needs

3. Fight back when criticized or challenged by my parent or by others

4. Can be defiant

5. React negatively to others I think are trying to manipulate me

6. Am not persuaded or not easily persuaded to do what others want me to do

7. Do not give priority to pleasing others or my parent

8. Do not try to soothe others' distressing feelings

9. Consciously do things I think will irritate or annoy the parent

10. Engage in challenging or provocative acts with the parent and with others

Add the fight reaction ratings to derive a total score. _____

Flight Scale

I...

1. Use silence as a defense against my parent

2. Sulk

3. Try to avoid interactions with my parent

4. Refuse to emotionally engage with my parent

5. Use passive-aggressive tactics, such as sarcasm, with my parent and with others

6. Refuse to engage in disagreements, even minor ones

7. Keep my thoughts and feelings private

8. Restrict responding or refuse to respond to the parent

9. Avoid conflicts

10. Am constantly on edge expecting attacks

Add the flight reaction ratings to derive a total score. _____

The category with the highest total score will be your characteristic response tendency. Review your responses on all three scales and make a list of the responses that you rated 4 or 5. These responses may be contributing to your distress or are ineffective, and may be negatively impacting your other relationships.

Joining Reaction

If the joining total score is your highest score, then this is your characteristic reaction. The joining reaction category describes behaviors that are associated with efforts to placate and please the parent. You do everything in your power to take care of the parent's emotional well-being and may even have the responsibility for that parent's physical care. You've experienced this reverse-parenting expectation, where you've taken care of the parent from your birth to now, and you may not be aware that there are other alternatives and options for relating to your parent. Further, you most likely act in similar ways with others—subjugating your needs and desires to attend to others' needs and desires, soothing others' distress almost always—and can be manipulated by others to do things you do not want to do or that are not in your best interests. There are many such carryovers that result from your joining with the self-absorbed parent. Other examples include the following:

- Adopting that parent's or other people's perspectives, opinions, and feelings, such as disapproving of someone because the parent or the other person disapproves

- Doing things others want you to do that are not in your best interests, because you need them to like and approve of you

- Assuming the responsibility to maintain harmony, even when it is not your responsibility or when doing so violates your values

- Anxiously scanning people to see if they are satisfied, need something, or are in distress

- Having a reluctance to disagree with or not ever disagreeing with someone, even in small or trivial matters

Joining is a response to the reverse-parenting role of the self-absorbed parent, where the child has to be the nurturer in the parent-child relationship instead of the parent assuming that expected role. The expected parental role is to nurture the emotional life of the child, attending to the child's needs and wants, and to respond empathically to the child. However, with reverse parenting, the parent is taken care of by the child.

The need to take care of the self-absorbed parent may be never ending, and you may unconsciously be extending this nurturing role to other relationships and parts of your life. For example, you may find that you take the responsibility for others' emotional well-being at the expense of your own.

Fight Reaction

Another possible response tendency is the fight reaction, where you refuse to assume the reverse-parenting role. It is easy for a child to become overwhelmed by the self-absorbed parent's needs, desires, and wishes, and to then have a defiant response to try to push away the parent in order to preserve the integrity of his or her own self. This response is one of refusal to comply with the parent's demand that the child take care of the parent's emotional needs and subjugate his or her own needs in favor of the parent's. The child can feel that something about the parent's demand is a danger or threat to the self, without a conscious awareness of what the danger is, and the fight response is triggered as protection.

The fight response is an aggressive one that is played out either actively or passively, or by some combination of the two. Active fighting responses include verbal refusal to comply with parental requests or demands, talking back in an effort to try to explain your perspective or position, initiating quarrels with the parent or with others, deliberate disobedience, and other such visible and active actions. There can be yelling, slamming of doors, stomping around and making a lot of noise, and engaging in other defiant acts.

Passive fighting responses can include all types of passive-aggressive behaviors designed to irritate your parent and show that he cannot control you. These acts include those that are in direct opposition to parental desires and preferences, such as refusing to participate in a sports activity that the parent chose for you, or choosing clothes, hairstyles, hobbies, or friends that differ from what the self-absorbed parent prefers for you. Other oppositional behaviors are sulking much of the time and starting fights with siblings. The goal is to keep the parent off-balance and away so as to prevent becoming overwhelmed by that parent.

As an adult, you can continue the fight responses, both aggressive and passive, and use these in other relationships and situations. The same defensive behaviors used in childhood are recapitulated in adulthood.

Flight Reaction

The urge to just get away from the self-absorbed parent forms the core of the flight reaction. You can physically, emotionally, and relationally flee from your parent, as you unconsciously fear enmeshment or being taken over by the parent and fleeing seeks to prevent this from happening. The self-absorbed parent perceives you as existing to serve and please him, and because you are a child and have not yet developed sufficient defenses or personal boundary strength, the flight response takes you away from the possibility of becoming enmeshed or overwhelmed. You can perceive the best strategy to be retreating from engagement when the parent is the most powerful and in control. However, while it may work to keep you away from your self-absorbed parent, this response can become habitual and extend to and present difficulties for your other relationships.

Flight responses include any type of withdrawal, such as zoning out, providing distractions, constantly dwelling on your thoughts or in your imagination, finding ways to be somewhere other than in the parent's presence, and simply not hearing or listening to the parent. You usually do not openly disagree with the parent or challenge the parent; seldom or never verbally fight with the parent; and do everything possible to withdraw, even in forced interactions with that parent. You do not try to soothe or placate the parent, as that would engage him or her; you emotionally leave. When these defenses are used by you as an adult, your relationships as well as your self-esteem can be negatively affected.

Another goal for this response can be to protect the true self from destruction, and so that self runs and hides. In its place, the false self that is presented can assume some of the behaviors and attitudes displayed by the joining and fight responses, and these are used to prevent detection and disclosure of the true self. This response and these goals can provide a lifetime of challenges for the child, who later has to search for the true self and, perceiving that others present the same threats as the parent, reacts to others by fleeing.

DIFFERENT RESPONSES AND OUTCOMES

Your total scores on the reaction scales in exercise 3.2 will probably indicate a higher total for one of the three response patterns, and that category should describe your typical responses to your parent and may also describe your behavior in other relationships.

Joining Response and Impact on You

When your highest score is in the joining category, you can experience some or all of these impacts:

- Idealization of that parent and unquestioning acceptance of his behaviors and attitudes

- An unconscious and unquestioning internalization of the parent's values, opinions, and attitudes

- A strong need to please that parent, no matter what the cost to you may be

- Constant vigilance to ensure that others' needs are always met

- A tendency to be or to feel manipulated or exploited by others

- Being perceived as nice, pliable, or compliant

- An inability to assert yourself when needed

- An inability to say no and stick to it

- Doing things that you do not want to do in order to fit in, maintain harmony, and the like

- An inability to relax for fear you will not notice something and then disappoint someone or others

You can be so enmeshed with your self-absorbed parent that you do not develop your individual self, differentiated from the parent's, and your sense of well-being and self-esteem are almost solely dependent on your parent's perceptions and approval. While there is nothing wrong with a desire to be like a parent or to adopt parental values and opinions, it is best for you if you can consciously examine and freely adopt these values and opinions, or have a choice about adopting them or not. When you consciously make your own choices, they then become yours.

Further, it is common and usual for children to want to please their parents and to make efforts to do so, but doing so can become troublesome when the major proportion of your time and effort is devoted to this, as you can never relax for fear of missing a cue from the parent that you need to attend to him. You may find as an adult that you are not only acting this way with your parent but also acting and feeling this way with other people. When parents are not self-absorbed or when they are less self-absorbed, this task of caring for the child is as expected, so the parents take care of the child's physical and emotional well-being instead of the child taking care of the parents' well-being.

The joining response can also be reflected in other parts of your life with other people, although you may not be aware that this is happening. Review the following to see if these behaviors and attitudes occur with other people in your world:

You...

- Have a deep desire to be liked and approved of by almost everyone

- Become very anxious when in the presence of minor disagreements

- Constantly wonder or fret that you've forgotten something that someone may want or need, even when it is not your responsibility to provide this

- Frequently do things that you do not want to do or that are not in your best interests, because someone wants you to do them or because you want to please someone

- Easily catch others' feelings, especially their uncomfortable or negative feelings

- Stay very alert to other people's signals of distress and try to ease these

- Constantly strive to be perfect and are never satisfied with what you do

- Almost always attend to others' needs and wishes

You may remain constantly anxious and on edge, fearing that you may not do what is expected for others, that you will not do it right, or that someone may be displeased. You may not develop your personal perspective, opinions, values, or independence. Even when you know that you are being manipulated or exploited by your parent or by others, you may feel helpless to prevent that from happening.

Fight Response and Impact on You

You fight very hard to prevent engulfment by the self-absorbed parent. It may feel at times as if the parent were trying to take you over, erase any hint of your individuality, and make you responsible for whatever the parent wants and needs, whether or not those wants and needs are clearly stated. You may feel that you will be loved only when you give up being a separate person from the parent. A difficulty can be that none of these thoughts and feelings are visible or spoken aloud. You may not even be able to formulate them in your mind to describe what you perceive is happening.

Your response is to fight off what seems to you to be an attempt to take you over and make you a part of the parent. But, because you don't understand what is happening and you cannot articulate your concerns, your actions to defend your self can be aggressive. It probably is not helpful for you to know that much of the parent's expectations are unconscious, which causes the self-absorbed parent to be unaware of how these unconscious but somehow communicated expectations are impacting you, but it is very likely the case. Neither of you understands the basic issues, as they are unspoken, but they are acted upon with some distressing outcomes for you. Some distressing outcomes for you can be the following feelings and perceptions that you carry with you:

- The parent is trying to make you into someone you don't want to be.

- You can never do anything that pleases the parent.

- The only way you can be accepted and approved of by this parent is to do and be only what that parent wants.

- Your parent seems profoundly disappointed with you almost all of the time.

- The parent makes unfair comparisons of you with others who are more pleasing to that parent.

- You stay on edge much of the time in expectation of parental demands.

- Your self-absorbed parent fails to hear or understand you.

- You must frequently act to defend your self from assaults by the parent or by others.

This is a defensive position, and you can feel that you are constantly under siege, as you are in danger of being attacked at any moment. Thus, you remain vigilant and alert to the possibility of assaults or demands from the parent. This position can be extended to others in your world: you are unable to assess the validity of your fears and perceptions about others, because you only have your experiences with the self-absorbed parent as a guide for assessing other possible threats; and based on those experiences, you have to be constantly on guard to the possibility of attacks.

The fight response to the self-absorbed parent can influence your responses to others in your world and can impact your interpersonal relationships in some of the following ways:

- You may keep others at a distance because you fear attacks on your self.

- In anticipation of possible attacks, you may go on the offensive and be aggressive, which also keeps others at a distance.

- You can be hypersensitive to any hint of criticism or blame, which produces an aggressive response.

- You can display a seeming indifference to the feelings of others, fearing that they expect you to take care of them.

- Since aggression can be your chosen mode of defense, you may unnecessarily provoke or challenge others, such as by teasing or taunting.

- Your suspicion of the motives of others can work to keep them at a distance.

- Your boundaries are so rigid that others cannot get to know you or get close to you.

- You can be constantly tense and anxious.

This reaction and the resulting behaviors and attitudes can cause you to have difficulty in initiating and maintaining meaningful and enduring relationships. Your fears that are associated with your relationship with your self-absorbed parent are unconsciously related to relationships with others.

Flight Response and Impact on You

Your fears of becoming engulfed, overwhelmed, or destroyed by the self-absorbed parent can result in the flight response to protect the self. The parent is perceived as being very powerful, demanding, and aggressive, and as having the resources to take you over. You, on the other hand, perceive yourself as helpless to prevent this from happening, and so you retreat by using some or all of these actions:

- Emotional disengagement

- Prolonged silence, a refusal to interact

- Sulking

- Becoming distracted and putting your attention elsewhere when someone is talking to you

- Forgetting what you agreed to do for the parent

- Daydreaming, zoning out, or thinking about there-and-then things when in the presence of the parent or others

- Becoming too busy with other activities, so you can avoid interacting with the parent

The flight response is one that removes you from perceived danger. You don't feel that you are powerful enough to fight off the self-absorbed parent's expectations and demands, most of which are unspoken, and you just want to get away from him. This perception of the parent and your responses can also be reflected in your other interpersonal relationships:

- You can be tentative and cautious with others, as you fear that they too are trying to take you over and you will be powerless to prevent this from happening.

- You may convey indifference or disengagement to and with others.

- It can be difficult for you to trust others.

- When your self feels threatened or in danger, you withdraw, become silent, or otherwise retreat.

- You stay in a constant state of anxiety, fearing attacks to take you over or to destroy your self, making it difficult or impossible for you to relax.

While fleeing can remove you from the perceived danger to your self, when this becomes a pattern of your behavior as an adult, you will find it difficult or impossible to develop and maintain positive relationships. Your understandable need to avoid becoming hurt or destroyed also prevents you from accepting potentially rewarding overtures from others who want to establish a relationship with you. You remain remote and safe from the self-absorbed parent, but this behavior also keeps others away from you.

WHY YOUR RESPONSE PATTERN MATTERS

The responses described in this chapter are general, and your reactions may not entirely fit into a specific category. However, your overall pattern of usual behaviors, attitudes, and feelings will most likely fit into one of these catergories.

The primary point of determining your usual response is to help you understand how your characteristic way of responding to your self-absorbed parent impacts how you behave with others and in other situations, and how this can even influence your perceptions of your effectiveness. Your characteristic response pattern may not be satisfactory for you, as you continue to experience negative feelings about yourself or your parent. Constant tension and anxiety can affect your physical and psychological well-being even if you have no conscious awareness of these effects. The chapters that follow describe strategies that you can use to manage your responses, protect your self from the destructive effects of the self-absorbed parent, have more satisfying and effective responses for difficult situations, and explore other positive self-development and growth alternatives.

As you embark on this journey, here is an exercise that can be helpful as you reflect on the troubling behaviors and attitudes of your self-absorbed parent. This exercise will help to prevent you from becoming upset or stressed as you continue reading this book, and can also be helpful when you have to interact with your parent, such as when he is critical or blaming of you. This exercise is perhaps most effective if you can draw or write as directed, but it can also be effective as a meditation without drawing or writing.

Exercise 3.3: A Safe Haven

Materials: For drawing, you will need one or more sheets of unlined paper and a set of crayons, felt markers, or colored pencils. For writing, you can use a computer, but it can be simpler to use just paper and a pen or pencil.

Procedure:

1. Find a place to work where you will not be disturbed and that has a suitable drawing or writing surface. Gather the materials you will need for drawing or writing, read through the next series of steps, and then follow the directions.

2. Sit in silence for a few minutes and allow an image to emerge that seems safe and peaceful to you. You may close your eyes or keep them open. Notice all of the aspects of this safe and peaceful place: sounds, sights, how you feel, and so on.

3. Once the image of a safe place is fully developed, use the paper to either draw or describe the image. You may want to list the feelings evoked in you as you look at your picture or read your description.

Whenever you are upset or distressed or are anticipating something unpleasant, such as an interaction with your self-absorbed parent, you may want to recall this image and allow yourself to become enveloped by the sense of peace and safety it evokes.

You now have three protective strategies, including the distract-and-discover (chapter 1) and emotional insulation (chapter 2) exercises, that you can employ to keep from becoming mired in distressing feelings. If you become distressed when interacting with your self-absorbed parent, you can then remind yourself of the picture of a safe haven or of the barrier you drew or use your emotional insulation. You can visualize the image in a second or two, and that will stop you from taking in any more of the parent's negative feelings, thoughts, or comments that are directed toward you. Thus, you can limit opportunities for you to have more negative or distressing feelings added to those you may already have. You can then become more reflective about the validity of the causes for your distress, thereby reducing the parent's negative impact on you. Using any of these strategies—distractors, a barrier, or a safe haven—provides you with a respite from continually taking in your parent's negativity.

SUMMARY

This chapter explored your reactions to the troubling behaviors and attitudes of your self-absorbed parent, both to help you better understand why you react as you do and to increase your awareness of how your customary reactions may not be helpful for you in the relationship with your parent. Three categories of reaction patterns were introduced to help you look at your own characteristic tendencies in some or all of your relationships, and to provide clues for how you can possibly make your responses more effective and satisfying. The next chapter provides some suggestions to guide you in how to change your thinking and responses.

CHAPTER 4

Changing Your Thinking to Change Your Response

Chapter 3 described some common responses to a self-absorbed parent and tried to categorize them so that the pattern of your usual behaviors and attitudes could be more readily visible to you. You may have developed a joining, fight, or flight coping strategy when you were very young, but this coping strategy is not sufficient for you to have the kind of relationship with your parent that you long for and that is less distressing for you. This chapter extends the discussion on responses and describes ineffective responses, ways you can make your responses more effective, and how to prevent some of the negative impact of the parent's troubling behaviors and attitudes on you so that you can be less distressed or upset. This chapter also presents some thoughts you may have that are not of help with your parental relationship or with your feelings about your self. Topics included are understanding that your hope for parental change is a fantasy, some usual but ineffective responses, the importance of not catching the parent's feelings, and strategies for managing your distress.

THE FANTASY THAT HOLDS YOU BACK

You may have a fantasy that your self-absorbed parent will become more loving as she ages because of your deep-seated need for a loving and caring parent. You may yearn and long for a parent who:

- Loves and understands you

- Perceives you as a worthwhile and unique person

- Attends to your needs and has these as a priority, at least some of the time

- Approves of and likes you

- Encourages and supports your strengths so that you grow and develop them

- Sees your perspective some of the time

- Refrains from criticizing, blaming, or chastising you

- Does not compare you with others to your detriment

- Does not taunt or tease you and then say that you are overly sensitive or can't take a joke, if you protest

- Acts as a nurturing and loving parent

The fantasy is that you imagine that you can do or say something that will cause the self-absorbed parent to change the negative behaviors and attitudes and become a parent who takes care of you. This fantasy can lead you to act in ways that are not in your best interests, increase dissention with your parent and maybe with others, engage in self-blame for not being good enough or able to please her, experience an erosion of your self-confidence and self-esteem, be too trusting of others or unable to trust others, and be exploited by your parent and by others.

It is difficult to accept that nothing you can do or say will cause your parent to change. This is not to say that the parent cannot change; it certainly is possible. However, it is unlikely that any change will happen until she makes a personal decision to change, which is an internal decision that she alone can make. The self-absorbed parent does not perceive any need to change, is unaware of the self-absorbed behaviors she displays, is indifferent or unaware of the negative impact on others, and is very well protected against any effort to reduce or eliminate these blind spots. For these reasons, it is unrealistic to expect that the parent will miraculously listen to you and develop a desire to be the parent you yearn to have. The energy that you expend on this futile effort could be more constructively and productively put to use in developing your self to become the person you want to be, to initiate and maintain satisfying and enduring relationships, and to work on increasing your appreciation and zest for life. While it is not easy to relinquish the fantasy, and doing so can take time and effort, giving up the fantasy can help you better cope with the negative effects of your parent's behaviors and attitudes. Giving up the fantasy can produce a number of benefits:

- Make you less disappointed that you seem unable to please the parent

- Considerably decrease the hurt when the parent puts you down, blames you, or criticizes you

- Lower your expectations for her expressions of love and approval so that you become less distressed when these expressions are not forthcoming

- Decrease your need to be defensive or to retaliate when interacting with the parent

- Result in fewer distressing and negative feelings

- Fortify your ability to resist the parent's and others' bullying

- Bring an end to berating yourself about your inability to do or say something that will cause the parent to change or to want to change

Giving up the fantasy allows you to accept your parent as she is, although the dream is hard to relinquish and doing so can take some time. However, if you tell yourself that it is your fantasy that you can cause the parent to change—and that wanting it to happen or trying to make it happen is a waste of energy and effort—then you can remind yourself of this whenever the parent does or says something that triggers your disappointment, hurt, anger, shame, or guilt. Becoming more realistic about your parent can also be a step toward healing and increasing your ability to cope with her troubling behaviors and attitudes. Although it can be difficult to accomplish, it can be a huge step in your journey to becoming the person you want to be, who is separate and distinct from your parent.

REDUCING INEFFECTIVE RESPONSES

Reducing or eliminating ineffective responses can be a first step toward increasing your effective responses. It is easier to provide effective responses after you become aware of how some responses are ineffective and then concentrate on eliminating them.

Change Your Characteristic Pattern

The first and maybe the biggest challenge will be for you to understand that your characteristic pattern for responding to the self-absorbed parent is ineffective. If your response pattern is in the joining category, you remain anxious and tense in the effort to prevent the parent from becoming upset and expend considerable time and effort in trying to anticipate and meet the parent's spoken and unspoken needs and wishes. You are taking care of the parent instead of the parent taking care of you, which would be expected. If fight is your characteristic response pattern, you can be anxious and tense, but it's because you can never predict when you will face a parental attack or assault. This anticipation keeps you on edge and can cause you to feel threatened, as you perceive that a threat or danger to your self exists, whether that perceived threat is real or imaginary. To prevent being attacked, you may also tend to attack first. The toll on your physical self and on your other relationships can be considerable. If your characteristic pattern is flight, you can feel lonely, isolated, or even alienated. In your efforts to avoid your self-absorbed parent, you can develop a habit of not allowing anyone to get close to you, and so you stay alone much of the time.

On the other hand, each category has some responses that you can adopt to become more effective. If your response tends to be joining or fight, you may find that the flight response of refusal to engage can be helpful at times. In other words, you may want to think about using a variety of responses from each category that could better fit a particular situation instead of just relying on your usual and ineffective response pattern.

How can you judge if a response is ineffective? A major guide can be your feelings and thoughts during and after you respond, such as the following:

- Your major negative emotion becomes more intense.

- You feel helpless, hopeless, or inadequate.

- You want to lash out or run away.

- You believe you need to try harder to be understood, but when you try harder, that does not work.

- You feel overwhelmed by the parent's feelings.

- You begin to feel guilty or ashamed without a good reason to feel that way.

- You berate yourself for not getting it right or not pleasing the parent.

You may want to become aware when you are continuing to use ineffective responses and work to reduce and eliminate these.

Avoid Challenging and Confronting Your Parent

Challenging or confronting your self-absorbed parent never works. This point cannot be overemphasized. Using either of these responses is not only ineffective but can also make you feel worse than you felt before. While you may perceive challenging or confronting as an effort to cause the parent to try to understand the impact of her distressing behaviors and attitudes on you, what is more likely to happen is that the parent will take what you do, see it as an attack, and quickly mobilize defenses. Your parent is most likely to have more defenses and stronger ones than you do. Remember that self-absorbed people tend to have certain characteristics:

- Hypersensitive to any perceived hint of criticism about themselves

- Well defended against any suggestion that they are less than perfect

- Alert to the possibility that everyone is set to attack their superiority because others are inferior to them

- Oblivious to the impact of their behaviors and attitudes on others

- Convinced that others are under their control and must do whatever they want or demand

These are some of the reasons why it is ineffective to challenge or confront your parent. If you are trying to get the parent to see her negative impact on you, you will not succeed, and your relations with your parent will be more cordial if you refrain from challenging or confronting her. Finally, if you want some more reasons to refrain from confronting or challenging your parent, just think of the times when you tried this. Did it work? Did you feel better afterward, or did you feel worse? Did your negative feelings persist? If confrontation or challenging did not work in the past, neither will be likely to work now or in the future.

Don't Catch Their Feelings

People who are self-absorbed can often be very powerful emotional senders, and other people can catch their feelings. To understand this concept, think of seeing a movie where the performance is so moving that you find yourself experiencing some of the emotions being portrayed, such as fear. Similarly, when you are in the presence of someone who is sad or depressed, you may experience a dampening effect on your mood—or, the reverse, when you are in the presence of someone who is ecstatic, you may become happy too. It's possible to catch the feelings of others, so your feelings are then influenced by those feelings that you catch. Neither the sender nor the receiver may be aware of what is happening between them, which can leave either or both confused about their emotions or the other person's reaction—or both.

Self-absorbed parents' emotions can be strong and intense and, when coupled with an internal and unconscious perception that their children are a part of them and are under their control at all times, can help explain some interactions that are troubling and distressing, especially for the child who is the receiver of the emotions and unconscious perceptions. Here's an example to illustrate how it can work:

Sender: The parent, who is grandiose, sees others as extensions of self, never sees self as making mistakes, and perceives self as perfect.

Receiver: The child, who receives projections because of insufficient boundary strength, does not yet have a fully formed self that is separated and individuated from the parent.

Sender's emotions: The parent becomes angry when the child, who is considered an extension of the parent and under the parent's control, makes a mistake. Making a mistake means lack of perfection, and that leads to the fear of being abandoned or destroyed. The parent wants to get rid of the anger and fear and projects these emotions onto the child.

Receiver's response: The child receives from the parent the projection of not being good enough, or of having made a mistake, and then internalizes this projection, which produces feelings of guilt and shame. This internalization and the resulting feelings can lead to a response of joining, fight, or flight, and the child can find it hard or impossible to let go of the negative feelings that were projected onto the child and internalized by the child, who believes these to be valid.

Neither the parent nor the child is conscious of most or all of the process just described. Neither is aware of the unconscious sending or receiving, which can be extremely confusing for the child, who is not able to screen out the parental projections. Over time, as many of these situations occur where the parent projects feelings or fears of not being good enough onto the child and the child takes in the projection and internalizes it, the child's self-perception and self-esteem is negatively affected and eroded.

So far, I've described how and why the child catches the parent's feelings. It is possible to prevent catching those projected feelings, but it takes some time and effort to develop preventive strategies. The best and most effective way to prevent this catching is for the child to develop sufficient boundary strength, to become more separated from the parent, and to develop an individualized self who is not an extension of the parent, no matter how the parent perceives it. All of this takes time and effort, and the material in this book can start this long-term process. However, there are some short-term strategies, and you are also encouraged to create some positive and effective strategies that suit your circumstances and personality.

The first step is to become aware that the parent may be sending negative emotions and that you are catching these. This will not be easy to do, as there can also be a realistic component, such as when you do make a mistake. It is not helpful for you to dismiss the reality and chalk it all up to the parent's self-absorption. Doing so can signal that you are like your parent in that respect, where you blame others, have to be perfect, and cannot admit to ever making mistakes. What can be more helpful is to admit the mistake if there really was one, but to not catch the negative feelings of not being good enough that accompany the projection. Step two is to employ your emotional insulation (as described in exercise 2.7), which can be very useful. You can hear the words, but the insulation can prevent you from catching the emotions. The image you created for your emotional insulation, such as the image of a feelings barrier, can be readily recalled at any moment. You can even bring it up in preparation for an interaction. For example, if your parent calls your name and you hear something in her voice that puts you on alert for a possible unpleasant interaction, you can immediately visualize your emotional insulation image, as the visualization takes only a few seconds.

The third and final step would be to assess how well using the emotional insulation worked. Did it feel as if you were less upset than usual in these interactions with the self-absorbed parent? If it was less upsetting than usual, then the insulation probably worked. If it did not work, revise the image to be stronger and more powerful. Words can be heard, but the projected feelings do not get through. In addition, ask yourself if it took as much time to let go of the negative feelings aroused in you. Are these fewer in number or less intense than usual? If so, the insulation worked, and you could use it in the future with the parent and in other circumstances to prevent taking in others' projections.

MANAGING YOUR DISTRESS WITH DISTRACTORS

Even if you are able to screen out your self-absorbed parent's projections, you can still feel some distress. The distress is worse when you have your own feelings plus the projected feelings from your parent. It may take some time before you can effectively screen out your parent's projected negative feelings, and you need a strategy to manage this until you are able both to screen out the projected feelings and to cope with your distressful feelings. The payoff can be that you are less upset in interactions with that parent or with other people and that you are able to more quickly let go of the distressful feelings that can linger after these interactions. Following are some ideas for managing your distress by using a distractor. There are five categories: physical, cognitive, creative, inspirational, and relational. First try an activity from each category and note which ones seem pleasurable. After trying these, you can adapt or modify the activities to fit your personality, as some may work better for you than others do. A bonus is that any or all of them can have the effect of enriching you.

Physical Distractors

The activities in this category are those that involve using your body to prevent getting lost or mired in negative feelings. By using the body, you have to attend to other stimuli, such as sensations, which takes you away from your negative thoughts and feelings. This is one reason why these distractors can work. So the task is to move, to become engaged in the activity, to concentrate and focus on what you are doing, and thus to be in the moment.

Exercise 4.1:   Physical Distractors

Find any necessary devices or equipment, and try at least two of the following: riding a bicycle, skateboarding, running, working out at the gym, yoga, flying a kite, cleaning up (room, locker, car, and the like), joining a pickup game, taking a stroll, dancing, jumping rope, pulling weeds.

As you do the chosen activity, pay attention to how you feel as you are engaged in it. Note any reduction in your negative thoughts or feelings.

Cognitive Distractors

Cognitive distractors use mental activities such as thinking, planning, mentally organizing something, and using your imagination (you may want to imagine a world of peace). Your thoughts can affect your feelings, and as you use this category of distraction, your energy moves away from negative or distressing thoughts and feelings. The examples in the next exercise have thinking as the primary activity along with some physical involvement, but other cognitive activities can also be used.

Exercise 4.2:   Cognitive Distractors

Get any necessary materials, and try two of the following: playing a video game, chess, card games, puzzles, reading for pleasure, working a crossword, Sudoku, counting (buttons, coins). Some of these can require a partner, or you can play on the computer.

Pay attention to your mood as you move your concentration to a mental activity. Also, try to see how long the mood persists.

Creative Distractors

Creative distractors can be very rewarding as these can produce a valued product as well as be distractors. You'll find that your engagement in creating distracts you from unpleasant thoughts and feelings, and you can also become interested, excited, and pleased during the process and for the product. There are opportunities to be creative in many parts of your life; doing so involves use of the new and novel, such as a new recipe for cooking. This category of activities can be a wonderful means for distraction and can also produce a product that can be enjoyed by you and sometimes by others. You may already have some creative pursuits that you can use.

Exercise 4.3:   Creative Distractors

Gather all of the materials you may need to use, such as paper, clay, canvases, paints or colored pencils, watercolors, crayons, a pen or pencil, cooking supplies.

Try a couple of the following: playing or listening to music, drawing, painting, sculpting, assemblage, scrapbooking, cooking, gardening, photography, collage, designing, writing. Pay attention to how you feel as you think about what you want to do, gather the materials, and perform the activity, and how you feel afterward.

Inspirational Distractors

Inspirational distractors are activities that can lift your mood and thoughts, get you out of yourself, and put you into the world, where you can appreciate yourself and others. These activities can distract you from a concentrated focus on yourself, your situation, perceived personal faults and shortcomings, and other such negative thoughts and feelings. In addition, they provide positives that you may be ignoring or overlooking, such as appreciation for others and for the beauty and wonder in your world; you can be altruistic and giving of yourself; and there is the possibility of you being able to make a difference for someone.

Exercise 4.4:   Inspirational Distractors

Do as many of these as you can:

- Help another person, such as a child with homework.

- Volunteer for community activities.

- Read an inspirational biography.

- Work at the local food bank.

- Coach a recreational sports team.

- Find a place of beauty and rest for a while.

- Use mindful meditation.

You may be able to think of other inspirational distractors that better fit you. These kinds of distractors can come from performing altruistic acts, where you give to others freely of yourself with no expectation of reward except the pleasure you derive from giving.

Relational Distractors

These activities can produce positive outcomes for other parts of your life as well as distract you from distressing thoughts and feelings. These are activities you engage in that are focused on enhancing and enriching some of your existing relationships and can also include initiating new relationships.

Exercise 4.5: Relational Distractors

Materials: A sheet of paper and a pen or pencil for writing

Procedure:

1. Find a place to work where you will not be disturbed and that has a suitable surface for writing.

2. Divide the sheet into vertical columns, enough columns for each friend or relative with whom you have a relationship you want to enhance, and write each of their names at the top of a column. If you want to initiate new relationships, just label those columns with "Friend."

3. Under each name, write an activity you could do with or for that person that you think would be meaningful for that person. These are some examples of activities: tutoring, teaching a new skill, doing the other person a favor, playing a game, joining in a community volunteer project, watching TV or a movie together, going for a walk, inviting the person to join you in a hobby or recreational activity, shopping together, having lunch.

Relationships take time and effort if they are to become meaningful and enduring. Also, building good relationships means that each of you is mindful and respectful of the other person. Being together and engaging in pleasurable activities promotes better relationships.

The important thing to remember for selecting your personal distracting activities is that these must be constructive and not harmful to you or to anyone else. Here is the final exercise to get you started on generating your personal list of distractors.

Exercise 4.6:   My Distractors

Materials: A sheet of paper with the following categories listed and enough space between the categories to write items or activities: pleasurable visual sights, energizing or soothing sounds, pleasing scents, wonderful tastes, skin sensors

Procedure: Find a place to work where you will not be disturbed. List several items for each category. The following provides some examples:

Pleasurable Visual Sights

- A field of yellow or colorful flowers

- The first snowfall

- Kites flying in the sky

- Kittens or cats playing

- Museum displays, especially those of glass

Energizing or Soothing Sounds

- Music

- Rain on the roof and window pane

- Children laughing and playing

Pleasing Scents

- Vanilla cakes cooking

- Roses

- Some lotions

Wonderful Tastes

- Coffee in the morning

- Pecans

- Strawberries and raspberries

- Crisp apples

- Popcorn

Skin Sensors

- The clean feeling after a shower

- Shampooing hair

- Silk clothing

It can be helpful to write some of your distractors on a three-by-five index card and carry it with you to have handy to remind you of distractors when you experience distressing feelings.

Continue to add to your list of distractors so that there are many ways to get out of negative and distressing feelings, help them to be less intense, and keep yourself more emotionally balanced.

MANAGING YOUR DISTRESS WITH AFFIRMATIONS

Other significant negative outcomes may be your feelings about yourself, an erosion of your self-confidence, and a decrease in your *self-efficacy*, which is your thoughts and feelings about your ability to constructively affect and manage situations you encounter. The blame, critical remarks, put-downs, and other negative comments directed at you by your self-absorbed parent can have long-term effects on your essential self in the process of development in the past or currently. Failure to meet the self-absorbed parent's expectations can produce feelings in you of shame for not being good enough, guilt for disappointing the parent, and deep and profound hurt to your essential self. These distressing feelings do not have to be internalized and accepted as true; they can be managed to reduce the long-term effects. In other words, you do not have to continue to feel ashamed, guilty, or hurt. You can recognize and accept your mistakes, a need for further development, and that no one can please everyone all of the time, and you can stop berating yourself for not being perfect or for failing to meet the self-absorbed parent's expectations. There are several ways to get to this point. One way to interrupt the distress you may feel when you are criticized, blamed, and the like is through self-affirmation.

Self-affirmation is a strategy to remind you of your positive attributes, skills, and strengths while, at the same time, you are working to grow and develop your self. Use the following exercise to start developing your list of self-affirmations, and when you are experiencing distressing feelings like shame and guilt, remind yourself of these positives by either thinking of them or reading the card (or however you've saved the list suggested in the exercise).

Exercise 4.7: Positives

Materials: A sheet of paper, two or more 3 by 5 lined index cards, and a pen or pencil for writing. You can also choose to do all of this electronically. The directions are for writing, and these can be adapted.

Procedure

Find a quiet place to work on this where you will not be distracted or disturbed by others.

1. Use the sheet of paper to make a list of your positive attributes, skills and competencies, and strengths, such as caring for others, being kind, showing resilience, acting thoughtful and polite, being imaginative, creative, and resourceful, showing others love and appreciation, and living in an organized and hopeful way.

2. Take one index card and select from your list in step 1 all of the attributes that describe you and write these on the card. Begin each with "I am..." These do not have to be in any particular order.

3. Take the other card and write down all of the skills and competencies you listed. Begin this list with "I can..."

Put the cards where you can easily access them when needed. Review one or both lists when you become distressed, especially after an upsetting interaction with your self-absorbed parent. The lists on the cards can be especially helpful when you feel blamed or criticized and when you experience self-doubt.

CHANGING YOUR THINKING

When you can do the following, you will have changed your thinking, especially about yourself:

- Give up your fantasy that your parent will turn around and become more loving and giving.

- Recognize and eliminate or reduce the ineffective responses you may be making.

- Institute barriers and insulation to prevent catching your parent's and perhaps other people's feelings.

- Create and use distractors when you are distressed and experiencing negativity.

- Resist confronting or engaging in useless conflict with self-absorbed people, including your parent.

- Accept the changes in the parent that come with aging and her responses to that inevitability.

While it is best if you can do all of the actions listed above, you will find that doing even one of them can produce major changes in your responses to your self-absorbed parent. You will have achieved greater separation from the parent, where you are no longer as manipulated by her disapproval and wishes as you were previously. Rather than catch your parent's feelings without consciously knowing what is happening, you will be able to take charge of the feelings you have and know that you control what you experience. You will find it easier to make adult responses when your parent is complaining, criticizing you or others, casting blame, and making other negative comments. Finally, responding appropriately to the parent will be easier as your distressing feelings will be reduced or eliminated, making it easier to think of good responses that do not upset either of you.

SUMMARY

This chapter focused on how to change your thinking, especially in distressful interactions with your self-absorbed parent. Part of your growth and development will be to recognize when and how you are continuing ineffective and distressing patterns of feelings, reactions, and actions begun in your childhood that may be contributing to your distress today, and to work to produce more adult patterns. Remember that you and your parent are both aging. While your parent will or cannot change, you can see the value of your changing to meet the new opportunities, possibilities, and responsibilities that come with your adult status. You can become your own person, and no longer will you be an extension of the parent; you can develop healthy adult narcissism, have meaningful and satisfying relationships, and, most of all, learn new ways to cope with your aging self-absorbed parent, thus eliminating or reducing the negative impact of her behaviors and attitudes on you. The next chapter continues the presentation of coping strategies.

CHAPTER 5

General Coping Strategies

Previous chapters focused on some actions to avoid and how to start the process of developing more positive aspects of your self, all of which will enable you to better cope with the aging self-absorbed parent's distressing behaviors and attitudes. This chapter presents some general coping strategies that may be helpful for any type of self-absorbed parent. You are encouraged to use those that best fit you, your parent, and the various situations you can encounter.

MANAGING AND COPING

The coping strategies in this chapter can help you better manage communications and other interactions with your self-absorbed parent, moderate some of the distressing feelings you may be experiencing, and provide you with a sense of having more control. Presented are some ineffective actions to avoid and suggestions for more effective actions. As you read these, you may find that some are more appealing than others, and you may want to consider all before selecting the ones you feel best fit you and your parent, as no one approach is sufficient.

Actions to Not Do

First examine those actions that you should avoid doing:

- Bringing attention to yourself
- Opening your self to the parent's projections

- Expecting your parent to understand and appreciate you, to be supportive and encouraging

- Expressing hurt, resentment, or other such feelings in response to the parent or in the parent's presence

- Having an expectation that others perceive or experience the parent as you do

- Displaying impatience, frustration, or other such feelings, either verbally or nonverbally

- Recalling events that portray the parent, you, your spouse, or your children in an unfavorable way, even when it may be humorous

- Chastising or criticizing anyone when the parent is present

- Indicating in any way that the parent is less than perfect, such as that he made a mistake

BRINGING ATTENTION TO YOURSELF

Your self-absorbed parent wants all of the attention most all of the time, so whenever you say or do something that deflects that attention, it can give the parent an opening to challenge, attack, or denigrate you. When you say or do anything, even as a comment or response, the attention can then switch to you triggering your parent's displeasure.

BEING OPEN TO PROJECTIONS

Be careful to not open your self to the parent's projections. Remind yourself not to maintain eye contact with him, orient your body toward the parent, or use other nonverbal behaviors that convey openness. Putting your emotional insulation in place before interactions with the parent is also helpful.

HAVING EXPECTATIONS

It is understandable that you will continue to long for your self-absorbed parent to change and become more loving and caring toward you, even when you are aware that what you long for is a fantasy that will not be realized. It's hard to give up that hope, but the constant disappointment you experience, in addition to the parent's distressing behaviors and attitudes, contributes to your distress. You are less likely to be disappointed when you don't have unrealistic expectations, and this helps reduce the distress for you.

EXPRESSING HURT

When you openly or nonverbally express that you are hurt, feel resentment, or the like—whether by what the parent said or did or by what someone else said or did—you are asking for the parent's understanding of the offense and reassurance of your worth and value. Your self-absorbed parent cannot give you empathy and is more likely to chastise or denigrate you in some way for your feelings. Reflect on your past experiences with that parent and see if you have ever had the reactions from him that you were seeking, an empathic response, or any positive response. The likelihood is that this has not happened.

EXPECTING OTHERS TO PERCEIVE THE PARENT AS YOU DO

Do not think or expect that others will perceive the parent as you do, even other members of your family. For example, your parent may almost always show you his grandiose side but show an impoverished ("poor me") side to others. You will see your parent's superior attitude: that others such as you are inferior, the need to always be right, and other such behaviors and attitudes. To others, your parent almost always shows his impoverished side—which emphasizes how he is unfairly treated and constantly being disappointed through no fault of his own—and expresses miseries and woes and other such complaints, so the grandiose side is suppressed. If others' perceptions are different from yours, then they will not react to the parent as you do or recognize your distress when triggered by that parent's comments or behavior. You cannot count on support or understanding from others, as that may not be forthcoming.

DISPLAYING IMPATIENCE OR FRUSTRATION

Using a poker face can be very helpful when you are in interactions with your self-absorbed parent, as any display of distress on your part can invite the parent to continue and increase his negative comments or attitude. It's not that you do not have these feelings, but it is best that you do not openly show them. Your parent is unlikely to sympathize, empathize, or cease distressing you. Your frustration and impatience can emerge because you're unable to get through to the parent. You never have been able to get through to him and have not fully accepted that you are unlikely to ever do so.

RECALLING EVENTS

While it may be tempting to try to show your parent as less than perfect by pointing out his past mistakes and flawed decisions, when you are in your parent's presence or when others are present, it will be in your best interests to not do this. Your parent can become enraged at any hint that he is not perfect and then turn it back on you. There is no good reason to recall these types of events for anyone, and for your parent least of all for many different reasons, the chief one being that you become less safe.

CHASTISING OR CRITICIZING OTHERS

You are cautioned to not chastise or criticize others, because your parent can use what you say to others against you, assist in criticism of the other person in ways that you did not intend to happen, or chastise you for your criticism of the other person. Refraining from criticism can be especially important for your children, spouse, or partner.

HIGHLIGHTING THE PARENT'S MISTAKES

Do not react to mistakes your parent makes in your presence unless those mistakes, such as misinformation, could result in harm to another person—for example, giving incorrect tax information. If you feel that the other person may be harmed in other ways, or that the matter is urgent and important, then take that person aside and correct the mistake. Your parent's grandiosity can prevent him from being able to accept public correction of a mistake, and he can go on the offensive against anyone who even suggests that he made a mistake.

Actions That Can Be Effective

There are some general actions you can take that will be effective, such as the following:

- Respond with sympathy and understanding—not empathy.

- Be patient.

- Use the feelings the parent projects onto you to understand what the parent is feeling, but do this only after you feel strong enough to screen out these projections when needed.

- Try to always be civil, formal, and courteous.

- When you have a request to make to the parent, do so in a firm, decisive manner with no explanations unless asked for.

- Become mindful of your nonverbal communication, and use clusters of gestures that will protect and defend you, prevent the parental assaults, and provide additional barriers.

- Minimize contact when possible.

- Develop a goal.

RESPOND WITH SYMPATHY

There may be legitimate reasons for providing sympathy and understanding, as the parent is likely to be experiencing some of the more distressing effects of aging, such as chronic aches and pains. You would extend courtesy and sympathy to others in those circumstances without receiving projections, and you can do the same for your parent. But sympathy does not mean empathy. You have been cautioned before about trying to be empathic with the parent. While you may value empathic responding, it is best if you save that for other relationships. What happens when you try to be empathic with your parent is that you open yourself up to your parent's projections of negativity onto you, and you are most likely to be susceptible to those projections and take them into your self, identify with them, and then act on those feelings, such as shame and guilt, by then experiencing them in addition to those you already have. You do not have to be empathic to respond appropriately to your parent's distress.

REMAIN PATIENT

There are many reasons for impatience, but it could be helpful for you to be patient with your self-absorbed parent, who is aging even when he may be denying that aging is taking place. Your impatience can stem from the unceasing complaining, casting of blame, disapproval of you, and lack of parental appreciation, and could also contain elements of your negative feelings about your parent. Whatever the reasons for your impatience, you will feel better about yourself if you can be patient and listen to some of what he says but not get caught up in his world.

SCREEN OUT PROJECTIONS

When you have strong and resilient boundaries, you can allow yourself to take in others' projections as a means of understanding what other people may be feeling. An example of this is what happens when you are talking with someone and start to feel angry, but you are unable to identify the source of the anger; you did not feel angry before, but something has triggered it for you. Since the sending and the taking in of projections are both done unconsciously, it may well be that what you experience is the projected anger of the other person that you took in. When you understand that this is what happened to you, do not identify and act on it by becoming angry yourself. Instead, what is more helpful is for you to note the projected anger, observe the other person to gauge his emotional state, and realize that what you are feeling is what that person is probably feeling. That is, the other person is angry and you caught it. Do not try to examine projections until you are sure that your psychological boundary strength is sufficient to recognize and resist those projections.

BE CIVIL, FORMAL, AND COURTEOUS

A positive coping strategy is to behave in interactions with the self-absorbed parent as you would in other important interactions in your world with people who are not in your intimate circle. You may have some negative reactions to the idea that your parent is not in your intimate circle. That parent may be a part of your intimate world, but this is a way to keep interactions with him from having a negative impact on you when the parent says things that provoke distressing and negative feelings in and about your self.

Civility, some formality, and courtesy in interactions almost always produce positive results. Your family members deserve the same considerations that other people in your life receive:

- Recognition of their individualism and as being separate and distinct from you

- Respect as worthwhile, unique individuals

- Appreciation for their value and worth

- Acceptance, tolerance, and so on

You probably extend these considerations to others as part of your professional and social life, but you may not recognize that these can also enhance your family life and can be coping strategies for interactions with your self-absorbed parent:

- Say "please" and "thank you."

- Ask if you can enter a person's room or sit down there; do not assume it is okay to do this even when the person is a child.

- Do not take or use others' possessions without first obtaining their consent.

- Be sure to greet the parent, as in "Hello, Mother."

- If you want to be very formal, address the parent as "Mother" or "Father."

- Try to not argue or disagree with your parent unless doing so is vital or important.

- Call before visiting. Do not just drop in.

- If you call the parent, always ask if this is a convenient time for him.

It is extremely difficult to object to polite behavior and verbal interactions.

MAKE FIRM REQUESTS

This strategy applies mainly to protecting your children, spouse, and others from the negative verbalizations and behaviors that some self-absorbed parents can display. Chapter 10 has suggestions for preparing your spouse or partner and your children for interactions with your self-absorbed parent, such as what to do when the parent says something that is demeaning to that person. You may need to intervene and ask the parent to not do or say something that is hurtful, and to do so in a firm manner is important. Do not be tentative when making these requests, although you would also have some concerns about being firm with your parent.

First, keep in mind that you are an adult and, as such, you are entitled to make adult-to-adult requests, although your parent may still relate to you as if you were a child and as if you were an extension of him. Also, it is helpful to remember to be polite and courteous as you would with others in your world, to keep your tone of voice calm and reasonable and your facial expression pleasant (unless the offense calls for looking stern), and to be clear and concise in your request. You can develop your own unique responses, but the following can provide some ideas:

- "Mother, I would appreciate it if you would not chastise _____. Let me know what needs to be taken care of, and I will do what needs to be done."

- "Father, please don't _____."

- For significant and important events and situations that will negatively impact a loved one: "Mother [or Father]. Do. Not. Do. That."

It is also important that you do not provide an explanation, unless one is requested, or volunteer a defense. Do not be put on the defensive when the parent protests that the offense was unintentional or that you are overreacting, but stay calm (or learn how to project calm when you feel differently), pleasant, and decisive.

NONVERBAL BEHAVIORS

This section focuses on your nonverbal behavior, which is usually more accurate than what you say. For example, when people say that they are "fine" but the facial expression, the tense body position, and the wringing hands say otherwise, they are most likely upset or distressed. The following are some suggestions for how you can use your nonverbal gestures or behavior to better cope with the self-absorbed parent.

Facial expressions. Do not wear your negative feelings on your face when interacting with the self-absorbed parent. When irritated, you do not have to frown, wrinkle your brow, or narrow your eyes. Maintain a pleasant expression, but do not smile constantly, as that can send a signal that you are not genuine. Pleasant neutrality is an expression that can be easy to maintain. Do not maintain eye contact with the parent, but do look at him. You can look at the parent's forehead just over his eyes, at his nose, or just beyond his ear. The parent may notice and make a comment about it, and at that point, you can shift to looking at his eyes for a nanosecond, but do not maintain sustained eye contact.

Body positions and orientation. Orient your body slightly away from the parent during interactions. Try to keep arms and hands relaxed. When standing, keep your feet slightly or widely apart as if you were rooted to the floor or ground. Try to maintain a balanced body position when sitting or standing. Do not slouch or become too relaxed in the parent's presence.

Strategic nonverbal barriers. Use strategic nonverbal barriers, such as magazines or sofa pillows, between you and the parent. You do not have to be obvious when using these, but they can keep you from catching some of the parent's feelings, give you time to center and ground yourself when under attack, and give you time to manage your facial expression.

MINIMIZE CONTACT

The effect of interacting with your self-absorbed parent may be so distressing that you may need to minimize contact, as that can keep you from constantly experiencing and trying to manage difficult and intense feelings. Contact is defined here as either face-to-face or by distant means, such as e-mails or telephone. Take inventory of how often you contact the parent and see if you can reduce these. You may be in a position where you feel that you have a responsibility to check on the parent to assess the parent's well-being, such as his physical condition, and minimizing contact is by no means suggesting that you do not fulfill this responsibility. Under these conditions, you do want to fulfill that responsibility, but you may want to find other ways in which it can be accomplished, without having to talk with the parent every time you check.

As an adult, especially when you have children, you can establish some family time to be at your home and not always go to your parent's home for holidays and celebrations. You could propose to visit every other year instead of every year. Another possibility is to shorten the visits and use the other time allocated for the visit as vacation time for your family. You can probably think of other creative ways to minimize contact.

DEVELOP A GOAL

The final coping strategy is to develop a goal so that you can more easily use the strategies provided in this chapter and to think of creating other strategies. The next exercise can help focus your efforts to cope by setting goals.

Exercise 5.1:   My Goal

Materials: One or more sheets of paper and a pen or pencil for writing, or you can use your electronic device

Procedure:

1. Find a place to work where you will not be distracted or disturbed. Sit in silence and reflect on a recent interaction with your self-absorbed parent.

2. Record the thoughts and feelings that emerge. Do not edit these or try to put them in any order. Just record them as they emerge. They do not have to be in complete sentences.

3. Review your list and place a T beside the items that are thoughts and an F beside those that are feelings.

4. Make two new lists, one composed of the items you labeled T for thoughts and the other composed of those you labeled F for feelings.

5. Next review these two lists and place an M beside each thought and feeling that was about yourself. For example, the thought could be *I made a mistake* (M); and a feeling could be *guilt*, which would also receive an M.

6. Now, place a P beside each thought and feeling that was about your parent—for example, the thought *He's being unreasonable* (P) and the feeling *He's infuriating* (P).

7. Count the number of Ms and Ps and decide which you want to have as a first goal: to reduce or eliminate the frequency or number of Ms or of Ps. A possible first goal could be one of the following:

   Reduce the negative thoughts about myself.

   Reduce the negative feelings about myself.

   Reduce the negative thoughts about my parent.

   Reduce the negative feelings about my parent.

   Or one of the following:

   Reduce the negative thoughts and feelings about myself.

   Reduce the negative thoughts and feelings about my parent.

8. Write your goal beginning with "My first goal is..." You may be tempted to have many goals, but it is best if you focus on having only one as your first goal. When you see some positive results for your first goal, that can be an encouragement for you to then formulate and act on another goal.

9. The final step is to write a means for assessing achievement of this first goal. For example, suppose your goal is to have some reduction of negative feelings about your parent. One way to assess that you have achieved this goal could be noting a reduction in the intensity of one or more negative feelings you usually have when interacting with your parent, such as feeling annoyed instead of being infuriated.

Seeing positive results or outcomes can take some time, but if you can persevere and remind yourself of your goal, you will be more likely to achieve it. Once you feel you are achieving your first goal, you can decide on the next goal. In addition, you will probably find that the steps you took to achieve your first goal can have a positive effect on the other possible goals on your list. For example, working to reduce negative thoughts could lead to reduced negative feelings, although that was not the original goal.

As you develop your goals, it could also be helpful for you to keep a journal about interactions with your self-absorbed parent, the strategies you implemented, and whether or not these were successful. Maintaining this record can keep you in touch with your successes and remind you to stop doing what was not successful.

SUMMARY

The general coping strategies covered in this chapter can apply to all self-absorbed people whom you may encounter. Their infuriating behaviors and attitudes do not have to continue to exert negative effects on you physically, emotionally, or relationally if you can use some of these strategies. Because these are general, you are also encouraged to create strategies that best fit your personality and situation. The next two chapters identify some strategies related to each type of self-absorbed parent.

CHAPTER 6

Coping Strategies for Clingy and Suspicious/Defensive Types

The first part of the chapter offers some possible strategies for the clingy parental type, and the latter part focuses on strategies for the suspicious/defensive type. All types of self-absorbed parents have an overlay of many of the effects of aging in addition to their self-absorbed behaviors and attitudes. The strategies presented here can be helpful in addition to the responses and strategies provided in chapters 4 and 5.

AGING AND CLINGY

Your parent may have always been the clingy type, but the parent's conscious and unconscious concerns about aging have increased and intensified these behaviors and attitudes. The next exercise presents a way to identify if your parent's clingy behaviors have increased. Reflect on the frequency and extent to which your parent currently exhibits the behaviors and attitudes in the scale.

Exercise 6.1: Clinging Behaviors Scale

Materials: A sheet of paper and a pen or pencil

Procedure: Find a place to work where you will not be disturbed. Use the sheet of paper to make a list of numbers from 1 to 8 for each of the following parental behaviors or attitudes. Rate the extent to which these behaviors and attitudes have increased in frequency or intensity in the past few years:

1—Neither intensity nor frequency increased

2—Intensity increased, but not the frequency

3—An increase in intensity and frequency

4—A significant increase in intensity and frequency

5—A marked and significant increase in intensity and frequency

1. Doing and saying things so as to retain almost constant attention from you or others

2. Complaining about minor things as well as major ones

3. Tending to whine

4. Engaging in actions to keep a youthful physical appearance, such as having an over-the-top number of cosmetic procedures

5. Exaggerating of aches, pains, or other physical discomforts

6. Conversations tending to center around how much she is suffering

7. Always or almost always needing something from you or others but does not openly or directly express what is wanted or needed

8. Insisting on daily or almost daily contact with you

Scoring

Add your ratings for numbers 1 to 8 to derive a total score. _____

If your total rating for your parent is 30 or above, she is becoming more clingy and is likely to continue.

Although you realize that some of the parent's complaints are valid, you may wish that these complaints did not demand so much attention, action, and feelings from you. Additionally, you may wish that the parent did not make these demands so often. It's like you are caught on a revolving wheel and cannot get off.

What can be more distressing is having to deal with your parent and your negative feelings at the same time. You may feel trapped and exasperated, but you may also feel some shame or guilt. Even if you have set limits on how much you intend to cater to the unreasonable demands that your parent makes on your time, and on how much you care for her, adhering to those limits can trigger your guilt or shame. And don't think that your parent will not use your feelings to manipulate you to get what she wants. Even when the parent's words seem to express an understanding of the unreasonableness of her expectations and demands, the parent's understanding is at best shallow and these are more likely to be words only being used as another way to manipulate you. This may sound like there is no way out, or that you will have to endure this quagmire forever. But the question becomes one of searching for what you can do to mitigate the negative effects on you and to preserve your integrity and self-esteem.

Again, you are cautioned not to challenge or confront the parent. You may be tempted to say something about the never-ending complaints, expectations of you, and the demands, but if you do so, the parent will consider that to be a challenge or a confrontation, in the sense that you are asking her to examine her behavior and its impact on you. This approach is unlikely to have positive results, as the parent can perceive your reasonable comments as being one or more of the following:

- A criticism of her

- Telling the parent that she is wrong in some way

- Your indifference to her suffering

- A way to get out of what the parent perceives as your obligations and responsibilities to her

- Ignoring the parent's feelings

- Making yourself the priority

- Ingratitude for all that the parent has done for you

While none of these may be valid perceptions, your parent perceives them as valid, and nothing anyone can do or say is likely to make a dent in the parent's negative and often inaccurate perceptions. If you can accept that your requests will not be received as intended, or as being valid, then you can begin to conceive of other ways to cope with the parent's clingy behaviors and attitudes.

Helpful Strategies for the Clingy Type

What follows are some suggestions to get you started on creating a set of strategies that are suited to you, to your situation, and to your parent:

- Provide soothing responses.

- Agree with her comments about suffering, and compliment her persistence in the face of adversity.

- Distract the parent when the carping, complaining, and the like persist for too long.

- Listen to the complaints, but do not try to fix the situation or provide solutions.

- Refrain from comments about the parent's physical appearance, mood, or the like.

- Do not minimize, ignore, or discount the parent's concerns.

Each of these strategies is explained in more detail.

SOOTHING RESPONSES

Soothing responses can be extended when it appears that the parent is upset or is in the throes of other intense emotions. These responses are intended to reassure the parent, to be calming, to lower the intensity of her feelings, and to provide relief. Reassuring responses are supportive and encouraging. These can be responses that reaffirm that there are personal or other resources available to address the event, concern, or situation. However, it is more important to pay attention to how you deliver the response than to the actual words.

1. It is important that you not catch the parent's intensity or distress. This can be done by instituting your emotional insulation.

2. Try to identify what the parent's feeling are, not the causes or the triggering event.

3. Breathe deeply before responding to provide additional calm for yourself.

4. Speak softly and slowly, but not too slow, and look somewhere in the vicinity of the parent's eyes; but do not maintain eye contact, as this could provide an opportunity for you to catch her feelings.

There are some common phrases intended to be soothing that should be avoided even when there may be some validity in using them. Avoid saying the following:

- "Calm down." Saying this to someone can be infuriating for the person.

- "Things are not as bad as they seem at this moment." Saying this minimizes, discounts, and invalidates the parent's experience. Even if true, the parent is not in a place where she can see that it isn't as bad as perceived, and it may very well be as dire or bad as it seems.

- "It could be worse." That may be true, but it is not responsive to what is happening now.

- "Things will get better." You cannot guarantee that will happen, and saying this is ignoring the current distress that is felt.

Most of these are platitudes, do not acknowledge the parent's feelings, and can be seen as discounting her experience. These comments have the potential for upsetting your parent.

BUYING IN

Even when you disagree with the self-absorbed parent, an effective response to the "poor me" attitude is to agree with your parent. It may not be true that the parent is suffering, that life is not fair, that she should not have to endure whatever is happening, and so on. However, it can also be true that there is little or nothing that can be done to remedy the situation. For example, it is not possible (yet) to prevent our bodies from aging, but that doesn't stop some people from complaining about it. This complaining, in turn, can be irritating to others, especially when coming from a self-absorbed parent, because the complaint can carry an unspoken demand that you, the child, are supposed to do something to prevent or relieve the circumstances of the complaint. You probably cannot do so, which can arouse your guilt and shame for not taking better care of the parent.

This coping strategy or response is termed *buying in* and is intended only to acknowledge what the parent presents as the parent's reality— that is, she is suffering and should not be suffering. The response is to verbally agree with that perspective even when you have a different viewpoint, wish that the constant complaints would cease, and understand that you cannot make whatever it is go away. Responses such as the following are noncommittal agreeing responses:

- "Gee, ain't it awful?"

- "It's too bad you have to suffer."

- "You'd think they could do something about that."

You may be able to think of other viable buy-in responses. You are also cautioned to not use the following:

- Responses that try to point out the reality of the parent's situation

- Saying something that suggests that the complaint is unwarranted, irrational (even when it may be), or illogical

- Suggestions for how the parent could help herself

- Suggesting that the parent could adopt a more positive attitude, perspective, outlook, or the like

- Asking questions about how you can help or what else can be done

Using any of those responses may arouse the parent's ire because these can be perceived as an indirect way of telling your parent that she is wrong, incompetent, illogical, and the like. Further, if you ask questions about providing help, you open the door to being asked to do things you do not want to do.

STRATEGIC DISTRACTING

Distracting as a strategy can be very effective when used wisely. However, its effectiveness diminishes when used too often or at the wrong time. The goal for distraction is to interrupt the self-absorbed carping, complaining, and the like, but first let the parent have an opportunity to vent some of her struggles, miseries, concerns, and so on. Interrupting too soon can lead to the parent feeling cut off, that you are indifferent or uncaring—all of which may have some validity but is not helpful for whatever relationship you have or want to have with the parent—and may produce conflict, which is best avoided as conflict seldom or never has the desired outcome for you.

Strategic distractions are those that try to move the parent from negative feelings to a thinking or cognitive state.

1. Begin with validating the parent's perceived situation—that she is miserable, has to endure adversity, or is unable to get what is wanted or needed—whatever the real situation may be.

2. Do not suggest alternatives, options, or ask questions about the situation.

3. After validation, give a comment about the parent's endurance, persistence, or any comment that seems to convey your understanding of her plight.

4. Move to asking questions first about the plight (but not too many questions, as that could tend to keep the focus on her misery), and carefully begin to comment or ask questions that are related but call for more cognitive, or thinking, responses.

5. Try to make the change of topic a gradual transition.

As an example, if the parent complained about a condition that is making her miserable, your response would be first to agree that the condition is limiting to her usual activities, next to ask if the condition prevented the parent from attending some usual event, such as a social club meeting, and then to ask questions about the social club, their plans, and so on.

LISTEN, BUT DON'T TRY TO FIX IT

It can be tempting to try to provide suggestions for how to fix the parent's problem. However, it is likely that you have in the past provided advice and suggestions that were intended to help but that the parent ignored, dismissed, and/or, worse, denigrated, which is ample reason to refrain from giving advice or suggestions now. In addition, do not tell the self-absorbed parent about your solutions to a similar problem or concern, and do not tell the parent about someone else who was successful or encountered a situation similar to the parent's. Although your intent is to be encouraging and helpful, it is unlikely to work and is more likely to irritate the parent, because the parent is focused on herself and cannot see similarities with you or with others.

Listening involves more than hearing; it also involves the following actions you should take:

■ Stop talking.

■ Focus on the parent, but do not maintain eye contact.

■ Do not interrupt or finish the parent's sentences.

- Hear the parent's words and feelings.

- Respond at appropriate times with a reflection of the content of what the parent is recounting, but do not try to verbalize what feelings you think the parent has.

- Ask questions only for factual information to clarify what was said, and restrict the number to one or two questions per conversation.

- Just listen.

It can be difficult to not try to "fix it," especially when you are confident that what you would propose will work. But, unless the situation is life threatening, you will be better off if you just listen.

AVOID COMMENTS ABOUT APPEARANCE

Do not provide unsolicited comments about the parent's physical appearance, not even positive ones. Aging brings many physical changes that can be distressing, and while the self-absorbed parent may be keenly aware of these, calling attention to them, even in a complimentary way, can be upsetting to that parent, who may then take this displeasure out on you. The self-absorption can cause the parent to be preoccupied with maintaining a youthful appearance, and she may go to great lengths and expense for maintenance, such as having many cosmetic surgeries. The parent's clothing can also reflect a preoccupation with maintaining a youthful appearance. No matter how you feel about what the parent is doing or not doing, it is best to not provide her with any hint of approval or disapproval—and the self-absorbed parent can detect even a slight hint of disapproval in the most innocuous comment you make.

It's best to confine your comments to those that do not call attention to physical appearance. Avoid saying "That color looks good on you" or "Nice sweater." Do not mention weight gain or loss, the new appearance of a hearing aid or other device that is supposed to be unobtrusive, inappropriate hair coloring or style, out-of-date or too youthful clothing, the disappearance of wrinkles or sagging skin, or anything that calls attention to the parent's physical appearance.

DON'T MINIMIZE THE PARENT'S CONCERNS

The clingy self-absorbed parent is likely to have and frequently verbalize numerous and varied concerns about health, finances, appearance, relationships, and so on. You can become weary of hearing the same concerns over and over, frustrated because you are helpless to fix anything, or feel inadequate because you do not seem to be able to meet your parent's expectations. Please keep the following in mind:

1. No one can ever fully meet the self-absorbed parent's expectations or needs.

2. When one concern is addressed, two or more other concerns emerge, so the concerns are never ending.

3. The parent is oblivious to her impact on others and especially the impact on you.

4. The parent's feelings of helplessness and fear are deep and pervasive but are not allowed to become conscious.

It can be helpful not to minimize, dismiss, or ignore the parent's expressed concerns. You do not have to agree with the parent's assessment of the concerns, buy into the possible dire consequences, or try to fix anything. (It's interesting that self-absorbed people do not seem to be able to perceive favorable outcomes, as doing so would relieve some of their felt distress, be encouraging and empowering, or bring less attention to them.) On the other hand, you don't want to encourage the parent to recount more about these concerns when they do not merit that much attention. There also may be some validity to the concerns, which you would not want to ignore. But if the expressed concerns are exaggerations, a bid for attention or admiration, or an attempt to keep you in line, it is still best to avoid saying anything that the parent could perceive as minimizing these concerns.

Helpful Actions

The following are some actions that may be helpful.

1. Provide sympathy and understanding, not empathy. Stay a little disconnected from the parent's suffering, concerns, and the like, but do sympathize with and try to understand her, as you would do with other people in your world.

2. Act with civility and courtesy. Treat the parent as you would a guest in your home or presence.

3. Be patient with the self-absorbed parent, as there may be more serious concerns, such as undiagnosed dementia, that cause some behaviors. However, do not respond to or treat the parent as you would a child.

4. When you make a request of the parent, ask for what you want in a clear, firm, decisive way, but do not provide explanations unless asked to do so.

5. Fortify your self with mindful meditation, emotional insulation, and self-affirmations, and the like before you interact with the parent.

By now you have probably thought of some additional strategies that you can try that will help make you feel less frustrated with your clingy parent or less guilty for not being able to ensure that the parent is always satisfied and comfortable, and that will help you feel more in control of your feelings.

The strategies presented in this chapter are intended to jump-start your thinking about what you can do differently that will fit your parent and your personality. Some of the suggestions may work as they are, some may be adaptable, and some may not work with your parent or may have the potential for worsening the situation for you. As you review the strategies, evaluate their usefulness for you, think of modifications, create different strategies, and prepare to use those that you think would be helpful.

THE SUSPICIOUS/DEFENSIVE TYPE

Certain strategies will work better with the suspicious-defensive type of parent, who can exhibit these characteristics:

- Takes little or nothing at face value

- Displays negativity toward you

- Ascribes deliberate neglect of her to you

- Is touchy, thinks that you and others are always being critical

- Demands perfection

- Is impervious to logic, reason, or change if it conflicts with her perception

- Questions you to extract every detail and demands extensive specificity about practically everything

- Seeks to manipulate and take advantage of you and others and is probably unaware of doing so

- Keeps a wall between herself and others

You can stay anxious and jittery around this type of parent and make the mistake of personalizing her negative thoughts and attitudes, as these seem to most always be directed at you. You are constantly being confronted with her displeasure. You may even go to great lengths to avoid doing or saying anything that would arouse the parent's displeasure, but that does not work, because it is an impossible task.

While it is unlikely that your parent will change and become less defensive and displeased, it is possible that you can lessen or eliminate some of the negative effects on you. This will take time and effort on your part, as you will be working on increasing your self-awareness and modifying your behavior at the same time. Increasing self-awareness refers to becoming conscious of some of your nonconscious thoughts, feelings, and attitudes. Modifying your behavior refers to assessing the efficacy of your behaviors to eliminate ineffective ones, trying new behaviors, and increasing the use of those that are effective.

The Parent's Goal

The suspicious/defensive self-absorbed parent usually has a conscious or unconscious goal to protect the self from being hurt or destroyed. This goal may be the result of the parent's previous experiences that began in childhood. It can also be important for you to remember that the parent can be unaware that she is acting on the basis of these earlier experiences, is oblivious to the impact that her actions have on others, and has an expectation that you know and understand all of her fears about being potentially hurt or destroyed. You are perceived not as being a separate and distinct individual in your own right but as an extension of the parent and, as such, under her control. You, on the other hand, are, or are trying to be, a separate individual with your chosen values, thoughts, ideas, and feelings, which are, or can be, different from the parent's. All of this can take place on nonconscious or unconscious levels for both of you. If you are tempted at some point to tell or confront your parent about any of this, please refrain from doing so, as it is not likely to be well received or understood. It is enough that you know and understand, as doing so can help you moderate the intensity of your negative feelings, especially those that you may have about yourself.

The primary goal of the suspicious/defensive self-absorbed parent can produce some or all of the following behaviors and attitudes for her:

- Constant vigilance and hypersensitivity to the surrounding environment

- Expecting hostile attacks, so everything is perceived as potentially hostile until it is proven to be otherwise

- Using attacks or attacking behavior as a defense

- Being very much aware of mistakes, errors, and the like, and missing positives

- Feeling that she is misunderstood most all of the time

- Being suspicious of others' motives

These suspicious/defensive behaviors and attitudes are very powerful and can make it uncomfortable to be around the parent who exhibits them. The parent questions the validity of everything almost all of the time and can cite many examples that she was correct to not believe what was said or done or meant. To get an idea of what the inner perceptions are like for this type of parent, just think of the hostile negative environments encountered every day by law enforcement, the IRS, and children living in an inner-city neighborhood where attacks can come from without and from within. Trust and safety cannot be expected under these circumstances, and developing protective mechanisms is critical to survival; these protective mechanisms become ingrained for ensuring personal safety. Your suspicious/defensive parent cannot see her world in any way other than hostile and dangerous. In addition, the parent may have relaxed the suspicion and lowered her defenses at some point only to be hurt or betrayed, which reinforced this need to be wary of others. Whereas many other people have similar experiences but can recognize that those were specific incidents, and not generalize them to everyone all of the time, your suspicious/defensive parent cannot make those distinctions.

Positive Strategies

Regardless of your usual response, you may be able to use some of the responses from the categories of joining, fight, and flight described in chapter 3 and those presented as general coping strategies in chapter 5. Review those for some ideas that fit your situation and your personality. Following are some specific strategies for the suspicious/defensive type:

- Do not try to change the parent's perceptions with alternative explanations or by focusing on the positives.

- Chatter about safe topics; provide details and be as concrete as possible.

- Do not present or talk about your mistakes or shortcomings or those of other people.

- Stay alert to signs of the parent's attempts to manipulate you.

- Use distractions.

- Admire her ability to see through deceptions and the like.

Be judicious in your choice of coping strategies and avoid using those that will make the situation worse, trigger intense feelings for either you or the parent, or tend to cause conflict.

KEEP RESPONSES NEUTRAL

You may want to try to change your parent's negative or defensive perceptions by pointing out alternative explanations that are positive but overlooked. This could be about you or about someone else. For example, the parent might make a disparaging comment about a relative who is having difficulty finding a job. You point out that this person is looking hard for work and recount the efforts the person is expending, only to have the parent then turn on you and pepper you with questions and comments about something you are not doing well, which is unrelated to the initial topic.

When you present alternative possibilities or explanations, your parent is likely to perceive this as you saying that she is wrong, and the parent cannot tolerate this. You do not have to agree with what the parent is saying; a better response is noncommittal or neutral, such as, "How about that!" or "Isn't that something!" or "Gee, who knew?" or "Oh my!" You can probably think of still better neutral responses.

CHATTER

If you must talk about something with your parent, chatter about a neutral topic, or ask about one of her interests, hobbies, or something similar. Ask questions designed to elicit information and encourage your parent to say more when describing something, but try to stay away from having the parent express feelings or opinions. Do not initiate discussions around topics where your opinions may differ from those your parent holds, as these can be opportunities for your parent to perceive that you are saying that she is wrong or ignorant. Differences of opinion and perspective are not well tolerated by this type of self-absorbed parent.

You may want to develop a list of topics to avoid.

Exercise 6.2:   Taboo Topics

Materials: A sheet of paper and a pen or pencil for writing; or you can complete this on the computer

Procedure:

1. Find a place where you will be free from distractions and intrusions. If you are writing, then you need a suitable writing surface.

2. Sit in silence and mentally review the interactions with your self-absorbed parent that occurred in the past six to twelve months. These interactions could have been face-to-face, talking on the telephone, or via other means such as texting or e-mail. Your review does not have to be in chronological order, and dates are not important.

3. As these interactions come to mind, write a list of the topics you remember being discussed.

4. When your list seems to be complete or is slowing down, look at each topic and give it a rating of P for positive, N for negative, or ? for neutral.

5. Develop a second list of all the topics that you rated as negative, and rate these according to the intensity of the negative feelings you experienced, from 1 to 10, where 1 is little or no emotional intensity and 10 is extreme emotional intensity.

6. Repeat step 5 for the topics you rated as neutral.

7. Place a check mark beside the topics that you rated as 5 or higher in each list. These are the topics that you want to avoid.

You may want to make a separate list of the topics to avoid, as this can help to reinforce these topics in your mind.

Exercise 6.3: Chatter Topics

Materials: A sheet of paper and a pen or pencil for writing; or you can complete the exercise on your computer

Procedure:

1. Review the first list that you constructed for exercise 6.2, and create a new list of positive topics as well as topics that you rated as neutral or negative that have an emotional intensity level lower than 5.

2. Review your new list to determine if there is a pattern for topics that are positive or neutral and that carry minimal emotional intensity. For example, you may see a pattern of topics related to the parent's hobby, current local events, a club or social organization, a TV show, or something that does not produce intense or negative feelings when discussed with your parent.

3. Once you have determined a pattern or the hint of a pattern, add to the list other possible topics that fit the pattern. You may end up with two or more topic patterns.

This new list can be your chatter topics. You can initiate conversations with these topics or extend a discussion on any of these if initiated by your parent or someone else. You can also divert conversations to one of the other topics on this list.

AVOID CONFESSIONS

It can be helpful to talk to people when you make mistakes or errors or to ask their advice or opinion about something you are contemplating. However, it is not helpful when the person then responds with critical or blaming remarks or put-downs that can be humiliating and add to your already negative feelings, and these are likely to be the responses of your self-absorbed parent. In addition, this type of self-absorbed parent never seems to forget mistakes you made in the past and adds to your distress by bringing these up in conversations even years later.

You may think that recounting your mistakes and the like is humorous or that others can learn from your mistakes, or you may be consciously or unconsciously seeking validation and support. However, when you recount mistakes in the presence of your parent, you give her an opportunity to make it a negative experience for you, to have her show that she is superior or to pile more negative feelings onto you. This is not a safe environment where you can openly admit or display your shortcomings.

RESIST MANIPULATION

This type of self-absorbed parent uses manipulation as a protection and defense and is poised to initiate it at all times. The suspicious/defensive type consciously uses manipulation, but other types can use it unconsciously. You are probably well aware of your parent's manipulation of you for her benefit.

Regardless of whether the manipulation is conscious or unconscious, it is being used to get you to act in ways that benefit the parent, although doing so may not be in your best interests, be what you want to do, or be in accord with your values or needs. The connection you have with your parent allows you to be more easily manipulated. This can be especially true if you are a caring and concerned person with a strong sense of responsibility, because your positive characteristics can lead to feelings of guilt or shame when your parent says or suggests that you do not care, are too wrapped up in other things or other people at the expense of the parent, or are shirking your responsibilities. While you know none of this is necessarily accurate, you can have your guilt or shame triggered just because it is your parent who is making the accusation.

The main strategy to prevent manipulation is to be very aware that your parent may try to manipulate you at any time. This awareness keeps you alert to the possibility, which can prevent you having your guilt or shame triggered because your parent is manipulating you to feel that you are a disappointment, not meeting his expectations, and the like. Another step is to recall typical remarks from your parent that tend to trigger your guilt or shame, and remind yourself to not react in this way when the parent again makes those or similar remarks. A helpful strategy is to use the parent's remarks as cues for affirmative self-talk. Affirmations such as the following can be helpful:

- *I do show caring and concern for her.*

- *I am good enough and don't have to feel guilty or ashamed.*

- *I will not be manipulated to do what someone else wants me to do. I can decide what to do for myself.*

- *I'm doing as much as I can reasonably do.*

It may take some time before you can stop having some guilt or shame triggered by your parent for not meeting her expectations at all times, but since that's an unreasonable expectation for you or for anyone else, it is up to you to decide what actions you want to take. When you arrive at the point where you feel that you can resist the parent's manipulation, you can act in accord with your decisions about what you want or choose to do.

DISTRACTIONS CAN HELP

If done subtly and not used too often, a strategic distracting process, as described in chapter 6, can be used with this type of parent. Since the suspicious-defensive type of self-absorbed parent can be overly sensitive to attempts to distract her, it may be more helpful to use physical distractions:

- Ask the parent to show or do something that involves moving to another location.

- Ask her if you can get her something, such as a drink or a pillow.

- Say that you need to check on something and leave her presence if only for a few minutes.

- Arrange in advance to have someone join you and your parent, so that changing topics will not be too obvious.

SHOW ADMIRATION

Everyone can respond positively to flattery, and this is another strategy you can use. Since your suspicious/defensive self-absorbed parent can be correct in detecting misleading or incorrect statements and even lies, you can flatter her ability to do this. Give your parent some credit for the use of this ability to uncover a questionable or an illegal act or to prevent being taken advantage of, since that could have led to dire results such as loss of money or being overcharged, being betrayed by a friend or colleague, or being manipulated by a supervisor or boss.

Disarming the parent with admiration may reduce some of the suspicious remarks directed toward you and also her defensiveness. Be careful not to pile it on too thickly or to belabor points, as doing so could trigger the parent's suspicion that you are not being sincere, which would negate your efforts.

SUMMARY

Coping with a self-absorbed aging parent can be very demanding of you, no matter what type your parent may be. The suspicious/defensive type can challenge you in many ways because this type is always on alert for hostile attacks, can seldom or never relax her defenses, and will go on the offensive as a protection. The strategies presented in this chapter, along with many of the general coping strategies in this book, can be helpful in decreasing the negative impacts on you.

CHAPTER 7

Coping Strategies for Arrogant and Belligerent Types

This chapter presents a further description of the behaviors and attitudes for the arrogant and belligerent types of self-absorbed parents, suggestions for actions to avoid with such parents, and strategies that can help you cope with them. These preventive and coping strategies are both to keep your negative and intense feelings from being aroused and to give responses that will not trigger the parent's ire. Both of these self-absorbed parental types can be aggressive and confrontational, and you will want to prevent these reactions toward you or your created family members.

THE ARROGANT TYPE

Some descriptors for the arrogant type include the following:

- Self-aggrandizing

- Contemptuous of people considered as lesser or inferior

- Constantly seeks attention or admiration

- Makes grand entrances and exits

- Centers conversations around self

- Overly proud of his accomplishments, status, or possessions

- Exhibits a very strong attitude of entitlement

- Charming, manipulative, takes advantage of others

- Expects or demands deference

The inflated self of the arrogant type is central to the description of the person, and although the inflated self coexists with the impoverished self, it is the inflated self that assumes the most prominence and is usually the one most often seen by others. It is not enough for arrogant types to build themselves up and act superior; they must also denigrate others and show them to be inferior. Arrogant parents can magnify any errors, mistakes, or flaws that others display but deny that they have any themselves. They believe that they never make mistakes, and when mistakes are made, it was because others failed in some way. Hence the mistake or error was really the other person's. The same kind of thinking goes along with any hint that the parent may have flaws. Anyone who thinks that the parent is flawed must be jealous and malicious, which makes the other person inferior. While it can be true that this type of self-absorbed parent has talents or special abilities, it also can be true that his self-perception is inflated and unrealistic, especially when accompanied with actions that are designed to show others as being inferior.

Coping strategies with the arrogant type of self-absorbed parent can become even more difficult for the adult child because of the effects of aging on the parent:

- They cannot deny the visible changes to their bodies or appearance.

- They may have to work harder just to maintain their usual level of performance.

- Other people start to have newer ideas, and these are more readily accepted.

- Colleagues, acquaintances, and other contemporaries move away, retire, or die, thus reducing their social connections.

- They may find it more difficult to form new social or work connections.

- It becomes harder to deny their lost opportunities, limited changes for the future, or the failure to achieve their dreams.

- Existential issues at the end of life and questions of life's meaning and purpose can become more urgent.

These are only some of the issues that confront the arrogant aging parent and can seem to make his worst behaviors and attitudes even more distressing for you and others. You'll need to remind yourself quite often that the arrogant self-absorbed parent cannot and will not change and reduce or eliminate his distressing behaviors and attitudes. You can, however, understand how these behaviors and attitudes affect you and initiate changes for yourself that can both help you better cope with your parent and moderate or eliminate some of the negative effects on you.

Helpful Strategies

Following are some strategies that can help. You are encouraged to adapt these and to create other such strategies that better fit your parent. Since you have lived and coped with your arrogant self-absorbed parent all of your life, you probably know that there are few effective actions or responses, but there are some: you can listen, as this parent is always eager to talk about himself; find something positive about the parent and flatter and compliment him; and assume an adult-to-adult stance for conversations, unless the parent is cognitively impaired.

LISTEN

The one topic that is always of interest to your parent is himself, so you can just about always count on something about the parent to be a central focus for almost every or for every conversation. The advantage is that as long as the parent is talking about himself, he is not making deprecating or other negative comments about you. This can be a positive for your interactions.

Listening effectively involves more than just hearing the content; it also includes understanding the meanings embedded in the content and providing an acceptable response. To listen effectively, you must first attend to the speaker by focusing on him and screening out other distractions. You can focus on your parent without maintaining eye contact, as doing that is not recommended; however, do not look around the room either, but try to keep your eyes in the general vicinity of the parent, such as focusing on his ear or just past it, his nose, or his forehead. Although you also may want to use distractions as a coping strategy, to listen effectively, you will need to screen these out. Try to hear the words and the underlying feelings that your parent is trying to convey, as these can be the most important part of the message. Doing so can help you formulate a response that is satisfying to the speaker. Do not try to feel what your parent is feeling, but use a more cognitive and abstract means to discern what is felt by him, as shown in the following example:

> Your parent recounts an incident where he gave someone incomplete information so that the person could not satisfactorily complete an assigned task, and he tells you about the increasing frustration expressed by that person. As you hear the words of the story, you pick up on the pleasure your parent feels about his actions that contributed to the other person's frustration; you have a sense that your parent feels that he is superior for being able to mislead the other person, that the other person is inferior for being misled, and that this incident has reaffirmed the parent's sense of self-importance. Your parent is taking pleasure in someone else's discomfort, to which he contributed.

You may be inclined to respond in a way that shows your displeasure about what he did; however, it is best to avoid the following kinds of responses:

- Disapproval of the parent's action

- Critical comments about the pleasure the parent feels at the other person's expense

- Empathy or sympathy for the other person's frustration

- Telling the parent what he should have done

- Directly or indirectly expressing your dismay or disgust

- Agreeing with his actions

- Acknowledging his superiority

Rather than respond in any of these ways, you can provide a neutral or noncommittal response that is still on topic. These responses are more effective under circumstances such as the one described, because you do not want to respond with any suggestion that the parent was wrong or that you disapprove of the parent, or that you agree with what he did.

Neutral or noncommittal responses could be asking follow-up questions or saying something similar to the following:

- "Tell me more about this."

- "You seem satisfied at the outcome."

- "You still have your edge."

- "You really know how to work the system."

If you notice, all of the examples keep the focus on the parent, as that is the one topic that is always of interest to him.

FLATTER AND COMPLIMENT

Since your arrogant self-absorbed parent is convinced of his superiority, you can never go wrong by providing compliments and flattery, if you are careful how you do so. You need to be careful about your tone of voice when delivering these, as you do not want them perceived as insincere or as sarcasm. Try to deliver compliments and flattery with a smile. Find something about the parent to use for compliments, such as doing something well, having a talent or skill, wearing something in a color that is flattering, or making a good selection, such as with decorating, buying a new automobile, or choosing a restaurant. Find something positive about your parent, and it will be easier to flatter and compliment him and to be sincere when you do. The following exercise will help you get started.

Exercise 7.1:   Compliments

Materials: A sheet of paper and a pen or pencil for writing, or a tablet or computer

Procedure:

1. Find a place to work that has a suitable writing surface and where you will be free from distractions and intrusions.

2. Think about your parent. If thinking about him produces negative thoughts or feelings, mentally push them aside for the time you are working on this.

3. Next think about the positive attributes and behaviors that you can associate with your parent. These can be just about anything: collections, hobbies, sports and recreation activities, organizing and planning, cooking. The possibilities are just about endless.

4. Record as many positives as you can think of at this time, and be specific. Examples for what your list might contain are "tells stories well," "has a pleasant singing voice," "can fix small appliances," "is neat and orderly in appearance," or "stays aware of what is happening in his immediate environment."

Your list of positives can now form the basis for what you say to compliment or flatter him.

You can use compliments and flattery to distract your parent and to move the conversation to more pleasant topics (it is very hard to be disagreeable to someone who compliments you).

ASSUME AN ADULT-TO-ADULT STANCE

Even if your parent continues to communicate and relate to you as if you were still a child, you do not need to continue to assume the role of the child in interactions with him. It will not be helpful for you to tell your parent that you are an adult, as he will not be able to understand and change, so resist trying to get him to change. You may need to be satisfied with just knowing that you are behaving like an adult in these interactions. When you can assume an adult-to-adult stance, your parent may be able to see that his parent-to-child stance is ineffective.

The first step is to become aware of how and when you act as a child with your parent, and when you assume the parental stance with him. Having to assume a parental stance with the arrogant type of self-absorbed parent may be infrequent, though this stance may become more needed as your parent ages. But, for now, let's focus on assuming an adult-to-adult stance with him.

An adult-to-adult stance requires that you interact with your parent as you would with another adult. If or when your parent communicates with you as if you were a child, resist the temptation to respond as if you were still a child, and try to respond from an adult's perspective:

- Avoid becoming angry, or hide your anger for the moment and do not let it show in your voice, face, or body.

- Refuse to react with shame or guilt to the parent's overt or implied criticism or blame.

- Respond matter-of-factly, with civility and courtesy, and with extreme politeness.

- Do not take what the parent says personally and become hurt. Even if the parent intended to hurt you, you can adopt an attitude that he must be referring to someone else and not to you.

- Use neutral responses that you would use with your boss or at a social gathering, such as "That's something to think about, but not right now," "That calls for some thought," or "I hadn't thought about that."

The most important thing is to not become upset or lash out as a child would. You would also want to refrain from becoming sullen or competitive with the parent or having other such childish responses.

THE BELLIGERENT TYPE

You probably want to just get away from the belligerent self-absorbed parent and to stay away. But for one reason or another, getting or staying away is not an option for you. This type of self-absorbed parent can be extremely unpleasant to be around, with few pleasant moments in his presence. Grumpy does not begin to describe this parent's usual mood or attitude. The image of a sleeping volcano comes to my mind as I think of this type of parent. It's at rest at present but could erupt at any time, spewing noxious gases and molten rock, and destroying any life in its path. With the belligerent type, it is almost impossible to predict an eruption and impossible to prevent or to contain one. The feelings of helplessness and dread are profound. Unfortunately, it does not help very much to understand that the parent has been deeply hurt, is hurting now, and has little or no insight into or awareness of the negative impact that his behaviors and attitudes have on others—and that this impact is the main reason he is avoided by you and by others.

Some Behaviors and Attitudes

Most distressing can be the parent's behaviors and attitudes that cause hurt to you and to others. It can seem as if nothing were ever right, acceptable, or pleasing to him; that he is not content unless discord and conflict are stirred up; and that he not only works to get others in conflict among themselves but also is combative and attacks without warning. This self-absorbed parent easily alienates others and is quick to take offense at almost everything. He is also extremely adept at carrying grudges. Aging will tend to expand and intensify these distressing behaviors and attitudes, so it will be helpful for you to be mentally and emotionally prepared for this event. This section will examine two characteristics of the belligerent type, envy and shallow emotions, to identify possible causes and to provide you with ideas about how you can determine how his other behaviors and attitudes could expand and intensify with age.

ENVY

While it is likely that your parent has always demonstrated envy, as the parent ages, this can become even more acute because of his conscious or unconscious awareness of the passage of time and the limits of his personal opportunities. Envy is defined here as the parent wanting what someone else has and feeling that the person has something that is undeserved, as that person is inferior to him. The self-absorbed person feels more superior and deserving, resents that what the other person has rightfully belongs to him, and begrudges any success, admiration, and the like that is bestowed on the envied person.

Envy is not limited to material things. It can emerge over any perceived advantage that the other person may have, such as the following:

- Talents and abilities that have their roots in genetics and were nourished and developed by the environment

- Happiness with family, friends, and accomplishments

- Wanted attention and admiration from others

- Status, whether earned, inherited, or bestowed

- Physical appearance

- Possibilities of opportunities and alternatives

- Meaning and purpose in life

- Mental, emotional, and physical health

Any of these can be possible targets of the parent's envy. The self-absorbed parent tends to focus on what others have that he does not have but thinks should be his, resent that he is being deprived of his just due, and feels that the world must be stacked against him or else he would have what is rightfully his. It is even worse for the parent when the child has any of these and the parent does not. The adult child can then become the target of the parent's envy. Complete the following exercise to determine if it is possible that your parent is envious of you.

Exercise 7.2: Parental Envy

Materials: A sheet of paper and a pen or pencil for writing, or a tablet or computer

Procedure:

1. Find a place to work with a suitable writing surface and where you will be free from distractions and intrusions.

2. Reflect over past interactions with your parent where he did any of the following, and make a list of the comments your parent made:

Was critical of your choices for work, family, vacation, car, and so on

Used put-down comments, especially about your appearance (for example, about as your nose or hair loss), abilities (such as lack of athletic expertise), or anything over which you have little or no control

Told you what you should or ought to do

Was dismissive or belittling of a success you had

Tried to take or took credit for your achievements and success

Be as specific as possible about the comments.

3. Look at the list you developed. Next to each item on your list, record something that you have that your parent might envy you for. For example, if your parent made a put-down comment about your height, you might write "physical appearance" beside that comment. You can refer to the previous list of possible targets of parental envy.

4. Review what you wrote and make a list of the possible characteristics or things that your parent may envy about you.

This exercise can give you some additional understanding of the source of your parent's negative comments toward you.

It is difficult to be the target of someone's envy, as you may not identify it as such, may try to cope with it and be ineffective, and may even start to berate yourself and feel inadequate. Further, the more you try to please the envious person, the more negative he can become toward you, leading to you becoming more confused about what is happening in your interaction.

SHALLOW EMOTIONS

One characteristic of self-absorbed people is having shallow emotions. Their emotions are limited in number, and those that they do have tend to remain on the surface. The only two emotions for them that are deeper and more intense are fear and anger. Self-absorbed people may seem to have the words for other emotions, but they do not experience them. They can make you think that they are experiencing an emotion when internally they do not. An example of this would be when someone acts as if he understood you were feeling hurt and says the appropriate words in response but then changes the topic or says something that lets you know that he really did not understand.

Shallow emotions are difficult to describe in terms of behavior, and it is likely that you will recognize the shallowness of the parent's emotions only in retrospect. There are a couple of indicators that could signal that someone has shallow emotions: the lack of frequency with which the person openly expresses emotions other than fear and anger, and the ease with which the person moves on from intense emotions.

Someone who has shallow emotions will have limited emotional expression and will infrequently express emotions that they do have. Anger is an emotion that self-absorbed people can easily access and express, so you will find that they express their irritation, annoyance, and other forms of anger often and readily. On the other hand, their experience of happiness may be minimal, if at all, so you seldom if ever hear them express appreciation, pleasure, or other forms of happiness. Other common emotions that can be shallow for the self-absorbed are sadness, guilt, shame, and love.

Another indicator of someone possibly having shallow emotions is the ease with which he can discard an emotion that he had seemed to be experiencing. The self-absorbed parent can quickly move on from whatever emotion was being expressed by him or by you. This capacity is what enables him to move from relationship to relationship so easily, because the caring, concern, or love was not actually felt—it was just words.

Helpful Strategies

Coping with the belligerent parent is a challenge. There is not much you can do to moderate the attacks on you. In addition, you may have been dealing with this distressing behavior all of your life, continue to hope that the parent's aging would bring positive changes, and find it difficult to accept that he is likely to become only more belligerent and aggressive with age. The following general suggestions can help, and you're encouraged to think of others that may fit with your parent. The most effective strategy is to avoid the parent, so you do not provide any opportunities for him to attack or verbally assault you and thereby trigger intense negative feelings. However, complete avoidance may not be possible for many reasons. For example, avoiding one parent could mean not seeing or interacting with your other parent, whom you want to continue seeing.

The most effective strategies begin with building and fortifying your self as protection; this is covered in chapter 9 because it demands an extensive discussion. Presented here are five actions that can help you cope better when interacting with your belligerent self-absorbed and aging parent:

- Expect attacks and rejection.

- Do not challenge or confront.

- Try to interact infrequently or at a distance, and to avoid one-on-one interactions with the parent.

- Do not openly disagree.

- Do not try to soothe.

Prevention is essential and preparing yourself for interactions is most helpful. Read the descriptions for each action and determine if it is possible or not possible for you.

EXPECT ATTACKS AND REJECTION

Since you have extensive experience with your parent, you know how he is most likely to behave and interact with you, which can be helpful. You can be braced for attacks and assaults, institute your emotional insulation in advance, and do what you can to fortify and protect your self from these. Expecting the usual belligerent behavior and preparing for it is much better than constantly being surprised and unprotected when it does happen.

DO NOT CHALLENGE OR CONFRONT

By now you probably know that it is futile and ineffective to challenge or to confront the parent, and that doing so can make matters worse. However, it is worth repeating, as this type of self-absorbed parent can arouse a desire to show the parent that he is mistaken, wrong, insulting, or the like. It isn't worth your effort to do this, as the parent will most likely become more enraged and assaultive. Your objective for challenging or confronting him will be lost, and the outcome most likely will be worse for you.

AVOID OR CREATE DISTANCE

If you cannot always avoid your parent, then try to make your interactions infrequent or at a distance, and do whatever you can to avoid one-on-one interactions with that parent.

Avoiding interactions is certainly helpful, but it also has a downside. First, avoiding your parent can produce some guilt or shame that you are not being a good child because of the desire to not be with your parent. This is a judgment about yourself that carries the assumption that you are supposed to sacrifice your well-being so that others will perceive you as good, or that wanting to be with your parent is expected of you, or other such messages that do not take into account your self-absorbed parent's behavior and its negative impact on you. You can be torn between wanting to live up to your desire to be a "good" child and the opposite desire to protect yourself from your belligerent parent, and this conflict can contribute to feelings of guilt and shame. The following exercise may help you sort through your feelings and thoughts to reduce your negative judgments and feelings about yourself that can be triggered by the desire to avoid your parent.

Exercise 7.3:   Conflicting Feelings

Materials: One or more sheets of paper and a pen or pencil, or a tablet or a computer

Procedure:

1. Find a place to work where you will be free from distractions and not be disturbed.

2. Close your eyes (if closing your eyes makes you uncomfortable, you can leave them open), and allow a past image to emerge of an interaction with your parent after you became an adult. There may be distressing feelings connected with the image, and if that happens, just open your eyes and record these feelings on your paper.

3. Record the statements that you recall your parent making to or about you during the interaction, and put a check mark by those that aroused the most distressing feelings for you.

4. Next record the major feeling you have as you review these statements. You may have more than one feeling. If so, record the most intense feelings that you have.

5. Review what you have produced thus far, and give each feeling you recorded a rating of 1 (little or no intensity) to 10 (extremely intense). You can also record and rate feelings you are having as you complete this exercise.

6. Go back to step 3 to reread the statements that your parent made. Review each to determine if the overt statement or the implication of the statement was one of the following negative comments about you:

"You cannot do anything right."

"You have so many flaws."

"You are lacking something."

"You always get it wrong, or you always seem to make mistakes."

"You are worthless."

Some of your parent's statements may have more than one negative comment about you, and you can also record these.

7. Now see if there is a pattern to these negative statements and comments by counting the frequency with which each appears. If "you are worthless" appears five times in your list while others appear only one or two times, then this signals a pattern.

8. Take the statement that appears to be part of a pattern and reflect on the extent to which you have evidence contradicting it. You could begin by writing down that the statement is not true and then list the evidence to support your position. Here is an example:

The statement "you are worthless" is not true because I...

Have a responsible job

Get good evaluations for my work

Pay my bills

Volunteer for community activities

Help my children with their homework

Attend to many of my parent's requests and demands

Am respected by my coworkers, spouse [or partner], and neighbors

The list can be long and serve as a reminder to you of your positive attributes and behaviors.

9. For the final step, write a paragraph that describes how you can reduce or eliminate much of the guilt or shame triggered by your self-absorbed parent's statements. For example, instead of letting those statements get through to you and be upsetting, you could use your statements in step 8 as self-affirmations before and during interactions with your parent.

Once you have a better understanding of how your parent affects you with his negative comments, you will find it easier to act so that the negative effects are prevented or can be diluted.

DO NOT OPENLY DISAGREE

You probably already know that it is futile to openly disagree with your parent, as you have learned over the years that open disagreement with anything your parent says only serves to enrage him even more, produce more intense assaults against you, and other such disagreeable outcomes. But it bears repeating here. You want your opinions and perceptions respected, and for others—such as your parent—to listen to and value these as you do theirs. However, this does not happen with your parent, as the parent still perceives you as a part of himself and, thus, under his control, which leads to the parent's conviction that you are supposed to be in sync with his thoughts, feelings, and the like and that you should not have any of these be independent of those that the parent has or holds dear.

In addition, your self-absorbed parent, because of aging concerns, is likely to become even more sensitive and touchy when encountering any hint that you openly disagree with anything he thinks or feels, as that can produce shame: shame that he is not powerful enough to prevent this from happening, that his self is not perceived as perfect, that his attempts to hide the flawed self were unsuccessful, and that, as a result, his self will be destroyed because it is now fully visible and seen by others as being flawed. Fear of destruction fuels the parent's need to attack and thereby defend the self by all means possible, and this includes defending himself from perceived attacks by the parts of himself that are represented by you, the adult child. Chapter 8 describes some ways to avoid openly disagreeing with your self-absorbed parent without having to give up a part of your integrity by always agreeing with the parent.

DO NOT TRY TO SOOTHE

Attempts to soothe the belligerent self-absorbed parent are most likely to be futile, and he can become even more disagreeable, leading to more distressful feelings for you. This parent can perceive your attempts to soothe as the equivalent of you telling him that he is wrong, inadequate, overreacting, shameful, childish, and so on. In addition, the parent does not see or understand the impact of his behavior on you or on others and is indifferent to your distress. It is very unlikely that this parent will be responsive to attempts to soothe, because in his understanding, the only correct perception and reality is the one that he experiences. The parent considers your personal reactions and feelings to be unrealistic, irrational, unimportant, and unworthy of his attention when they seem to differ in any way from his. Therefore, it can be best not to try to get this type of parent to relinquish his defensive attacking and belligerent behaviors.

SUMMARY

You now have some possible strategies to use with four types of self-absorbed parents. Each parent can be self-absorbed in a different way and have a different impact on his children, who also differ from each other. Therefore, no one strategy fits every parent. In addition, your personality and other characteristics will determine how comfortable you are with any of the suggested strategies. Please consider the strategies presented in chapter 6 and in this chapter as starting points for developing your own set of personal strategies that work for you, that are consistent with your personality and values, and that fit your situation. Chapter 8 relates to all types of aging self-absorbed parents and is particularly relevant to coping with the belligerent type, as it addresses how to manage conflict and assaultive confrontations.

CHAPTER 8

Managing Conflict and Assaultive Confrontations

Your self-absorbed parent may tend to provoke conflict, both with you and between you and others. Some self-absorbed parents, especially the belligerent type, can also engage in assaultive confrontations, where you face a barrage of blame, criticisms, and other denigrating and demoralizing remarks. You may not be expecting either conflict or confrontation, which can leave you undefended, hurt, and angry, without being able to manage or address the charges or your feelings. You may feel even worse when your parent does this to members of your created family.

Aging concerns can make these distressing behaviors become more frequent and intense, as the parent can be increasingly concerned and fearful about her ability to manage and survive in the future. Cranky, grouchy, and miserable do not adequately describe them, but these descriptors give you an idea of how some parents can react to their aging concerns. What is more distressing is that these parents then displace these feelings onto you and others, as they do not understand or accept that they are not in control of their aging outcomes. Since you, as their child, are unconsciously considered to be an extension of them and under their control, they expect you to fix their problems and concerns, and they can be angry when they perceive that you are not doing so. Although this expectation is unreasonable, it is also unconscious for these parents, so they just act on it by attacking their adult children.

As aging changes are gradual, you may not be fully aware that these changes, and your parent's unconscious expectations for you, may be fueling her increased provoking of conflicts and assaultive confrontations.

This chapter proposes that your perspective about conflict and confrontation can contribute to your reactions, gives suggestions for how to manage your reactions, and suggests some effective responses to conflict and confrontations.

HOW YOU PERCEIVE CONFLICT

Many people dread any type or level of conflict, and you may be among them. Some people become anxious at any hint of conflict, even when it may be mild, such as a disagreement. The dread and anxiety may come from the perception, fear, or experience that conflict is always hurtful and destructive. Some conflicts do fit this description, but not all conflicts have to be destructive. There can be some positive outcomes, and these will be presented later along with some strategies that you can use when anticipating or engaging in conflict with your self-absorbed parent. Let's begin with an exercise that will help you clarify how you think and feel about conflict.

Exercise 8.1:   My View of Conflict

Materials: Two or more sheets of paper, a set of colored pencils or crayons or felt markers, and a pen or pencil

Procedure:

1. Find a place to work that has a suitable writing or drawing surface and where you will be free from distractions and disruptions. Have the materials readily at hand, and read the remainder of the procedure before beginning to work.

2. Sit in silence and allow yourself to settle down and become calm. You can close your eyes or leave them open.

3. Breathe deeply for a few seconds. Then think about conflict and allow an image of conflict to emerge. The image may be a real or an imagined scene, an abstraction of shape and colors, or a picture

of something or someone. Do not edit or change your image. Notice as many details about the image as you can.

4. When you have examined your image, open your eyes (if they're closed) and draw your image.

5. Record your thoughts and feelings about your image and about your experiences as you allowed the image to emerge.

6. Review both your image and what you recorded in step 5. Reflect on the following questions and record your answers: What is the central thought or feeling reflected in your image? Is this the central thought or feeling you have in interactions with your self-absorbed parent or when you anticipate having to interact with her? Is this the same thought or feeling you have in interactions with others?

7. Write a summary statement or paragraph about your image of conflict, the major thoughts or feelings you experienced, and how all of these relate to interactions with your parent and with others.

8. The final step is to identify your goals for future interactions with your parent in conflict situations. The goal has to be about you, it has to be realistic, and it must not require that your parent change. Here are some examples:

■ *Reduce my negative feelings about myself.*

■ *Do not allow myself to "catch" my parent's anger.*

■ *Learn what to do and say to reduce the number of conflicts with my parent.*

■ *Explore ways to prevent conflicts from escalating.*

The examples may give you some ideas of how you can phrase your goals to be specific enough so that you know when these are achieved and to be realistic enough to fit you, your parent, and situations that can emerge. However much you may want to eliminate conflicts with your parent, this may be unrealistic given her self-absorption. You can be more in control and feel better if you can be more effective in conflicts and assaultive situations.

Common Reactions

It also may be helpful for you to explore the common reactions people have to conflict and to determine the characteristic responses that your parent exhibits as well as the ones that you display. Presented here are seven common behaviors used in conflict situations: avoid, soothe, agree, challenge, force or attack, manipulate, and compromise.

Avoid. This conflict behavior refers to taking actions to prevent becoming engaged in conflicts. Such actions can include leaving the person's presence at the first sign that there may be conflict, providing misleading statements, giving false information or omitting information, and other such evasive acts.

Soothe. Attempts to soothe are made by providing suggestions that, whatever the conflict is about, it isn't that bad, that things will get better, to look on the bright side, and other such statements. This is done to try to intervene and prevent the other person from expressing her negative feelings or from having these feelings become more intense.

Agree. Agreeing with the speaker may diffuse the conflict and reduce her negative feelings. While this is best used when it can be sincere, there may be times when insincere agreement is effective, especially when it is done in a way that is not sarcastic or easily detected as being insincere.

Challenge. This behavior is a cognitive or emotional presentation of another perspective to try to get the other person to support a different position or opinion. This may be effective to get the other person to think about what she is saying, but it can also be delivered in a manner that suggests that the other person is wrong, stupid, ignorant, or hopeless. When done in that manner, it becomes a form of attacking behavior delivered in such a way that any protest can be easily dismissed or denied.

Force or attack. There is no doubt in anyone's mind when this occurs, as the attacker is forceful, persistent, determined, and may even speak rapidly and loudly. Even when the tone and voice are not loud, the attacker's word choices and interruptions convey her hostility.

Manipulate. This behavior can be used in conflict situations to seduce, coerce, or persuade the other person to agree or to appear inept and wrong. Your positions and arguments are manipulated by this person so that you find yourself in a position where you have to agree with what she says or reject your own values. You are manipulated to be in agreement or to be defeated.

Compromise. Compromising behavior demands that both parties respect and are able to understand each other's position or viewpoint. In addition, both of you work to try to get to a place where you can agree on the important points and are willing to differ on the less significant ones.

Exercise 8.2: My Usual Behaviors in Conflicts

Materials: A sheet of paper and a pen or pencil, or the exercise can be completed on a computer or a tablet

Procedure: Create a list of the common conflict strategies previously described: avoid, soothe, agree, challenge, force or attack, manipulate, compromise. First rate the frequency with which your parent uses each strategy, and then rate the frequency with which you use each strategy:

1—Uses this never or almost never

2—Uses this infrequently

3—Uses this often

4—Uses this very often

5—Uses this all or most all of the time

Evaluate the effectiveness of the strategies that you rated 4 or 5 for your parent, and do the same for yourself. This information will be the starting point to consider changes for your strategies in conflicts with the parent.

Competition Needs

Another way to look at conflict behavior is from the perspective of the level of competition needs for your parent and for you. Competition needs can be mild or intense, vary within a person depending on the situation, or be interwoven with one's personal self-perception and self-efficacy. Competition needs can be expressed in many ways, such as the following:

- *I'm better than others.*

- *I'll show you.*

- *It will be devastating if I do not win.*

- *I can beat [or overpower] you.*

- *I must not lose.*

- *I'll use any means necessary to win.*

There is a positive side and a negative side to competition. When used positively, it becomes a motivator to exert more effort to achieve and improve, whether in sports, at work, in training and education, or any other situation. Positive competition needs can be encouragers to do more and better, such as to study harder, to train and condition for a position on a sports team, or to seek ways to increase sales.

The negative side to having competition needs arises from the intensity with which people allow them to overpower their thinking and behavior. Winning is then the primary objective for all aspects of their lives so that they devote their time and energy to winning, use any means possible to win, are indifferent about the impact that these behaviors and attitudes have on others, and are consumed by the intense need and desire to win. Strong competition needs can lead to unwise decisions, impaired relationships, and general dissatisfaction with oneself for not coming out on top in everything.

You may want to examine your parent's and your personal behavior in conflict situations for the level and intensity that competition plays in these conflicts for you and for your parent. Do either of you have to best the other or feel as if you lost or are inferior if you do not? Do conflicts tend to escalate because neither of you is willing to compromise or stop before the conflict gets to a highly tense point? Is it possible that your competition needs—the only ones you can control—play a prominent role in conflicts with your self-absorbed parent? Working to make your competition needs positive or constructive can help you reduce the number of conflicts with that parent and maybe even with others, reduce the negative impact that these conflicts can have on you, and increase your feelings of self-efficacy. If you have strong competition needs, use these wisely for situations that are important and significant and not for those whose outcomes will be minor or insignificant at best. If your self-absorbed parent has strong competition needs, remember that nothing you can do or say will change that parent.

Conflict Outcomes

Your usual or main behavior for conflict will work some of the time, but most or much of the time you may not be satisfied with the outcomes or your residual feelings. The following exercise will help you gain some insight into how you may be able to become more effective.

Exercise 8.3:   My Feelings After a Conflict

Materials: A sheet of paper and a pen or pencil for writing, or a computer or tablet

Procedure: Reflect on how often you experience the following feelings after a conflict. Create a list of feelings and rate how often you have these feelings after a conflict:

1—Never or almost never

2—Seldom

3—Frequently

4—Very often

5—Always or almost always

Feelings

Each feeling has other levels for that feeling.

Angry: includes annoyed, frustrated, irritated, furious, and rage

Resentful: includes hurt and vengeful

Fearful: includes dread, terror, and panic

Confused: includes disoriented, off-balance, and feeling manipulated

Guilty: includes remorseful, anguished, and self-reproachful

Shamed: includes embarrassed, regretful, and disgraceful

Sad: includes dejected, disconsolate, and miserable

Satisfied: includes pleased, glad, and gratified

Calm: includes peaceful and serene

Energized: includes excited and upbeat

Review your ratings and determine how many of the rated feelings were positive and how many were negative. Most likely you rated the first seven feelings (angry, resentful, fearful, confused, guilty, shamed, and sad) higher than the last three (satisfied, calm, and energized). The first seven are intense negative feelings, and the last three are more positive. The last three feelings could be your goals for working to increase more effective responding and reacting to conflicts in general, but especially to those that occur with your parent.

It will be reaffirming of your self-efficacy to be able to have one or more positive feelings after a conflict and to have fewer or less intense negative feelings. Both are good reasons to examine your conflict behaviors, review ones that might be more effective, try one of more of these (called *behavior rehearsal*), and continue to assess their effectiveness.

RESPOND MORE EFFECTIVELY

You can be more effective in conflict situations with your self-absorbed parent by doing the following:

1. Changing your behavior and attitudes

2. Relinquishing the desire and efforts to change your parent and to have her understand and accept your perspective when it differs from hers

3. Developing your inner self to be better protected from the negativity of the parent (this is addressed more fully in chapter 9)

4. Reflecting on your competition needs to see if they are helpful, or if they are working for you

5. Establishing goals for what you would like to have as outcomes for conflict situations with your self-absorbed parent

6. Learning to assess the significance and importance of the conflict to make a better choice of a strategy

7. Determining your parent's goal for each conflict

Changing your behaviors and attitudes will provide you with a foundation that will assist you in implementing your chosen strategy for conflict situations with your self-absorbed aging parent. Changing the behaviors and attitudes that intensify your distress—such as trying to reason with the parent or needing to win at all costs—can significantly increase your effectiveness.

Relinquishing the desire to change the parent has been mentioned several times, but it bears repeating, especially for conflict with the parent. It's your desire or longing that contributes to your distress. If you can simply accept your parent as she is, recognize her positive and negative attributes, and understand at a deep level that she is unlikely to change as you would desire her to change, you will have made monumental steps toward managing yourself in conflict situations, as you will no longer have an unobtainable goal.

One step that you can take early on is to reflect on your competition needs and evaluate how these are helping or hurting your effectiveness. It's not that you need to give these up, as they may be working well for you in some venues, but you may want to be more judicious in selecting where and how to let them motivate you, and not let them cause you to act in ways that are not in your best interests. For example, if you are highly competitive, you may want to win all of the time, which can be helpful in your work or career. However, you may want to reflect on how this intensity and focus on always winning has impacted the relationships that mean the most to you, and determine if some of your relationships would be better served if your need to win was not so strong all of the time.

Establish a goal for yourself and try to stay focused on it during and after conflicts with your parent. You may even want to practice using that goal in disagreements or other minor conflicts with others. Suggestions for goals include the following:

- To remain calm, speak softly, and try to see your parent's perspective

- To not try to convince or persuade her that she is wrong or inaccurate

- To not have residual negative or distressful feelings, such as anger or fear

- To prevent catching the parent's feelings or other projections

Whatever goal you choose, be sure to be realistic about what you can do and what you can hope to change about yourself to be more effective. Making small changes can be effective, and it can be affirming when these work.

Not all disagreements are significant ones, nor are all disagreements important unless you perceive them as such. Learn to assess these aspects to better understand when it is necessary to resist becoming involved. You do not need to take on every conflict with your self-absorbed parent, nor are all of these conflicts important to your well-being and health. Begin to ask yourself in every conflict, *How important and significant is this to me and to those I care about, and do I need to take it on? Will the outcome be worth the effort I will have to expend?* Some conflicts will be important and be worth your efforts, while there are others where the costs will outweigh the benefits. Choose the best strategy based on the answers to those questions.

The final suggestion is for you to try to determine your parent's goal for the conflict. Goals for the parent's behavior could be one or more of the following: attention getting, revenge, admiration seeking, to win and be superior, manipulation, self-defense in anticipation of an attack, and/or displacement.

Understanding your parent's goal assists you in choosing the most effective coping strategy. For example, if the parent's goal is revenge for an imaginary offense, or a real offense as she perceives it, then choosing a strategy that addresses that goal will be effective.

COPING STRATEGIES

Some of the strategies covered in chapter 9 to protect your self can also be useful in conflict situations with your aging self-absorbed parent, and vice versa. The six coping strategies presented here are avoid, soothe, agree, refuse to engage, delay, and reflect back. The first three were covered briefly as common coping strategies and are expanded on in this section. You may already be using one or more of these strategies, but with your added understanding of how to respond more effectively, along with a greater awareness of your parent's goals, and by adopting a variable conflict-management approach, you can use these strategies more effectively.

Avoid. This strategy involves avoiding the parent in the effort to not participate in the conflict. You probably have more than one technique that you use to avoid your parent but you may not think to use it in conflict situations. It could work here. You can also avoid introducing topics that you have reason to believe could lead to a conflict with the parent, such as child-rearing practices, political issues, or any perspectives that differ from your parent's.

Soothe. When you use this strategy, you are trying to reduce tension, usually for the other person but sometimes also for yourself. You use words, phrases, and a tone of voice intended to be calm and reassuring. However, do not say anything like "Calm down," as that is likely to have the opposite effect and can be infuriating.

Agree. This strategy is similar to soothing and has the same intended outcome, to relieve tension either for yourself or for the other person. You can use phrases like "I agree that you have a point there," "I see it like you do," "It's nice to be able to agree on this," and other such phrases when these are true and do not compromise your principles or integrity.

Refuse to engage. This strategy is an act of resistance where you simply do not take the bait and engage in the conflict. You can say something like "I don't want to get into that" or "This is not the time or place for that discussion," or you can change the topic, leave the room, or use other such evasive techniques.

Delay. This strategy can be of help when the timing of the conflict would be disruptive or upsetting to you or to others or when engaging in the conflict is inappropriate for the current situation, such as at a party. In this instance, you could say something like "Let's save this discussion for later."

Reflect back. This strategy uses a form of intellectual, understanding responding where you reflect back to your self-absorbed parent what she is saying, meaning, and feeling. You do not try to be empathic, as that would open you up to taking in her projections—for example, feeling her fear, making it yours, then acting on it and finding it difficult to relinquish—and you do not want to do that. Reflecting back just calls for you to be detached enough to recognize the content of what she is saying and the feelings directly or indirectly expressed.

Variable Conflict-Management Strategies

Variable conflict-management strategies rely on your level of emotional intensity (EI) and the significance and importance (S&I) for you of the topic that is central to the conflict. Those two considerations produce four quadrants:

I. High EI, high S&I

II. High EI, low S&I

III. Low EI, high S&I

IV. Low EI, low S&I

HIGH EI AND HIGH S&I

It is usually best not to engage actively in conflict when your emotional intensity is high, as your emotions make it much more difficult for you to mentally reason and to maintain control. However, when the significance and importance are also high, you may need to address the topic, as it may affect your well-being or the well-being of others in your life.

Suggested strategies are delay, avoid, and refuse to engage if possible.

HIGH EI AND LOW S&I

Just as for quadrant I, when your emotional intensity is high, it is usually best not to put yourself in a conflict situation, as your emotional intensity may cause you to say and do things that you could be sorry for afterward. The outcome will be undesirable for you, and your emotional intensity may increase. When emotional intensity is combined with low significance and importance, that becomes another good reason to let conflict go for the time being.

The best strategies are to delay and avoid.

LOW EI AND HIGH S&I

This state of low emotional intensity and high significance and importance is the ideal setting because the topic has significance and importance for you and your emotions are more under your control. This allows you to think more clearly; you will be able to be rational and logical. You can be more effective in assessing your parent's emotional and cognitive states, determine her goal, and use this information in a constructive way. You may even be able to come to a compromise, providing that it will not violate your principles or integrity.

Use any of the six suggested coping strategies, depending on your parent's state.

LOW EI AND LOW S&I

If neither emotional intensity nor significance and importance are high, there is no good reason to engage in a conflict.

Two strategies to use are agree and soothe. In addition, you could also use the strategies of distract, drift, and neutral responses (covered in chapter 9).

SUMMARY

The discussion on managing conflict focused on helping you understand what you can do to reduce your distress, contain and manage your difficult reactions and feelings, and better understand the factors that may be a part of your parent's behaviors and attitudes during conflict. The information suggested a process and strategies that can help you cope better with conflict. Chapter 9 continues with what was presented in this chapter by proposing ways you can protect your self, whether in a conflict or not.

CHAPTER 9

Protecting Your Self

Your self may have been subjected to many psychological injuries that were inflicted by your self-absorbed parent throughout your life. You did not or may not have many of the psychological resources that prevent such injuries. The main emphasis of this chapter is to guide you to an understanding that you do have some resources that you may not recognize or use, and to provide suggestions for additional resources. This chapter leads you to developing positive self-affirmations, building and fortifying your inner self, developing strategies for how to manage intense emotions, and preparing for parental assaults and attacks. The chapter also proposes strategies you can employ as protection when you are in interactions with your parent.

OLD PARENTAL MESSAGES

The chapter begins with an exercise that summarizes some of the old parental messages that you've internalized, that you may believe about yourself, or that may have unconsciously affected some of your behaviors, attitudes, and relationships. The exercise encourages you to create positive affirmations about yourself. The goals are to make you aware of how those old parental messages continue to affect and influence you and to help you to further build your protection from your self-absorbed parent, whose negative behaviors and attitudes toward you may have intensified and worsened because of the influence of his aging concerns.

The exercise has two parts, and I'm using a plant metaphor for guiding your thinking. First think of your self as a plant struggling to grow; the first part of the exercise helps to clear away the weeds and underbrush so that the roots can breathe and take in nutrients. The second part shows you how to provide the self with what it needs to grow and thrive.

Exercise 9.1: Old Parental Messages Updated

Materials: Two small current photos of you or a collage of images and symbols that can represent you today, two sheets of cardstock, double-sided tape or a glue stick, crayons or felt markers for drawing, and a pen or pencil for writing

Procedure:

1. Gather all materials and find a suitable place to work, with a hard surface for drawing and writing and where you will be free from distractions and interruptions.

2. Begin with selecting one sheet of cardstock and attach one of the photos to it in the center of the page. Or if you do not have a photo, draw or glue images and symbols to represent yourself today as a collage in the center of the page. (Whenever a photo is referred to in later steps, you can use this collage or a copy of it.)

3. Close your eyes and reflect on the parental messages you received about yourself through the years that continue to linger today. These messages can be about your physical appearance, your intelligence, how you please or displease the parent, your achievements, your talents or lack thereof, measuring up to expectations, how you compare to others, your athletic abilities, and your value and worth, or there may be other messages that you recall hearing or sensing.

4. After reflection, open your eyes, select a variety of crayons or felt markers, and quickly record in one or two words each of these parental messages about you around the photo or central image.

5. Next, on that same page, record the *shoulds* and *oughts* that you recall hearing the parent say about or to you, such as "You ought to know what I want."

6. Review what you wrote, and then write a summary statement about your product on the back of the cardstock. This ends the first part of the exercise.

7. Take the other sheet of cardstock and a photo, and tape or glue the other picture in the center.

8. Using the crayons or felt markers, write your positive attributes around the photo using different colors for the variety of attributes you possess. Examples for positive attributes include imaginative, creative, optimistic, intelligent, thoughtful, persistent, playful, reliable, caring, organized, resilient, abstract, concrete, talented, determined, cheerful, or any positive characteristic about you that comes to mind.

9. Write a summary statement about your positive attributes on the back of the cardstock.

10. Remove your photo or image from the page that has the negative parental statements and discard that page. Keep the page of your positive attributes in a place where you can refer to it.

Take a little time to look at your positive attributes, and congratulate yourself on the positive way that you've developed to this point. You may have more work to do on your self, as we all do, but appreciating what you do have is also helpful.

The remainder of this chapter will present information and ask you to participate in exercises that will aid you in developing your protective strategies, guide you in handling parental attacks, propose a strategy for healing your narcissistic injuries, and discuss how to build your inner resources. There are two parts to protecting your self. First, you will find it helpful to reinforce your inner self. This involves repelling bad stuff, learning not to personalize, managing panic, and choosing your emotions. Second, you will prepare for attacks and assaults (which may be either direct or indirect) by learning different protective actions to take.

REINFORCING YOUR INNER SELF

A strong and resilient inner self is critical to prevent further injuries caused by your parent's negative actions toward you. You have been subject to what is called *narcissistic injury* from an early age, where your essential self was wounded. Most everyone suffers these injuries. While difficult to heal, some injuries do heal or are resolved; others can be repressed and denied, and some can remain subject to reinjury, especially by your self-absorbed parent, who probably provided many of your earlier injuries. However, you can reinforce your inner self to withstand parental and other attempts to reinjure you or to inflict new injuries.

But how can you reinforce your inner self? The long-term way is to build your psychological boundary strength so that your parent's negative comments and the like do not injure you. All of the exercises and activities in this book are designed to guide you in that process but they are not sufficient alone. You may also need or want to work with a competent therapist, who can help you resolve lingering family-of-origin issues and other unfinished business from past experiences, as well as assist you in becoming the person you want to be. What this chapter can do is illustrate how you can protect your self, which is a short-term strategy to use while you are developing and reinforcing your inner self. Following are four suggestions for reinforcing the self: repel bad stuff, do not personalize, manage panic, and choose your emotions.

Repel Bad Stuff

This strategy helps you cope with parental blame, criticisms, put-downs, unfair comparisons with others, and other such actions that can be hurtful. Repelling does not mean that you throw these back on the parent and blame, criticize, or denigrate him. Doing that is likely to lead to additional attacks, open conflict, and other such negative outcomes. It does mean that you take care to initiate your emotional insulation—a shield, mirror, or other protective image—so that the parent's negative comments do not reach you. Visualize the parent's negativity toward you as one of the following:

- Ice arrows that melt before they reach you

- A thrown baseball that falls in front of the parent, like when a small child tries to throw a ball that fails to go the distance

- Rubber nails that bounce off of your emotional insulation

- A strong wind diverting the words and blowing them away

- Thrown stones that pile up before they reach you, thereby building a wall between you and your parent

You can probably think of other visualizations that would repel the bad stuff.

Do Not Personalize

Another protective and reinforcing strategy is to teach yourself how to not personalize your parent's blame and other negative comments that are directed toward you. Yes, the parent does mean to blame, denigrate, and criticize you, but there is nothing that requires you to accept, buy into, believe, or act as if the parent's comment were true. You have the power to internally reject those negative comments about you.

You may be asking yourself how it is possible to not personalize the parent's comments when there may be some truth, or an element of truth, in what the parent is saying, such as when the parent criticizes you for making an unwise choice or decision and you have to acknowledge that possibility to yourself. But suppose that the parent did not stop there but went on to say that you are inept, incompetent, and other such negative designations. Under these circumstances, you can acknowledge to yourself that the choice or decision was unwise and make a vow to yourself that you will do better next time, and leave it at that. You do not have to accept the negative terms the parent directs toward you or acknowledge anything out loud. In addition, you can mentally do some or all of the following:

- Visualize the product you constructed about your positive attributes in exercise 9.1.

- Recall some of your self-affirmations.

- Forgive yourself and pledge to do better.

- Design a plan for doing better next time, such as analyzing the mistakes and imagining tactics you can use.

- Think positive thoughts about yourself.

You will want to be realistic and not deny that you make mistakes or that you need more personal development, but you also do not want to buy into your parent's negativity. Just because you made a mistake, are not perfect, or can do better does not mean that you need to continually beat yourself up or allow someone else to do that. You can focus on the positives you have and work on those parts of yourself that still need work.

Manage Panic

Some people can panic when faced with a blaming and critical parent. Panic is an emotion that has intense bodily sensations that accompany it. Sensations such as a racing and strongly felt heartbeat, an elevated pulse, tense muscles, disoriented or chaotic thoughts, and a dry mouth are preparing the body to fight or to run away. It may not be unusual for some people to panic when their parent begins to chastise, blame, or criticize them. They can perceive that their self is under attack and is in danger, but are unable to assess the extent and validity of that danger.

Following is a process that could be helpful in any situation where you feel panic:

1. Stop. Briefly stop your thoughts and body. Become immobile for at least a nanosecond.

2. Ask. Ask yourself if you are dying or in immediate danger of dying. If the answer is yes, take immediate action to protect yourself. If the answer is no, proceed to step 3.

3. Notice. Notice if anyone else is dying. If so, seek help, provide assistance, and so on. If the answer is no, take a deep breath.

4. Institute calming actions. Make a conscious effort to calm yourself, further appraise the situation, and assess the validity of the felt danger. Calm yourself by breathing deeply, slowing your thoughts, and relaxing the most tense parts of your body, and reflect on the question, *What's the worse that can happen to me right now?* If you or someone else is not in danger of immediately dying, you have time to think of the appropriate actions to take, assess if the perceived threat is as dangerous as you first thought, and then act.

Using this process gives you a structure to assess if your reactions are realistic for the circumstances. Thinking, assessing, and breathing help you to manage what you feel and do in intense situations that are not real crises.

Choose Your Emotions

The final strategy is to reinforce your self by choosing your emotions. You may think that you are powerless over your emotions, as these just seem to arise within you without your conscious awareness. It's true that you do not have complete control, but you may be able to lessen your distress and intensity by choosing what to feel in those moments with your parent when you seem to have the most negative feelings.

But first, you have to be sure that you are aware of what you are feeling. Can you stop for the moment and identify your current feeling? What are you feeling right now? Is identifying your current feeling easy to do, or do you find it difficult to identify a particular feeling? You may have several feelings all at the same time and find it difficult to sort through these to identify any one feeling. If so, try to identify the major one, the one with the most intensity. You may not be able to identify a feeling and may find that you focus on sensations, or you may be vague about what you are experiencing, such as feeling uncomfortable or upset. If you are having difficulty, you may want to practice being aware of your feelings in the moment and defining them.

DEFINING FEELINGS

Feelings begin with a collection of sensations. For example, body or muscle tension, rapid heartbeat or pulse, clenched teeth, racing thoughts or paralysis of thoughts, and hands curled into fists could be a collection of sensations that signal that you are angry. There are also gradations of feelings like these for anger that range from irritation at the mildest level to annoyance, to anger, to fury, and finally to rage at the most intense level. You will feel differently at each of these levels. A dictionary or thesaurus can provide you with words and descriptions to help you identify the range of feelings connected to other common feeling words, such as "sad," "happy," "fear," "shame," "guilt," "despair," or "remorse." Try to practice more accurately identifying your feelings, as that can help you choose what you want to feel. For example, instead of becoming angry, you could become aware of when you are irritated and take steps to keep your irritation from escalating to anger.

Once you are aware of your feelings at any particular time, it will become easier for you to analyze what you are experiencing and feeling and to assess the validity of that feeling for a particular situation. For example, anger prepares the body for fight or flight from perceived danger, so when you notice that you are angry, you will want to ask yourself, *What is happening that I consider as dangerous?* and *Do I need to prepare for fight or flight?* If you answer yes to the second question, then the feeling you have is consistent with the circumstances. If the answer is no, this gives you an opportunity to sort through your other feelings and choose to feel one that is more in line with the situation.

NEGATIVE FEELINGS

You probably feel some of the following when interacting with your self-absorbed parent:

Shame: feeling fatally flawed, that you are not good enough

Guilt: feeling that you disappointed the parent, failed to live up to expectations; that you are not acting in accord with your values

Anger (includes fury and rage): feeling that you are being unfairly judged, discounted, dismissed, or disparaged

Fear: feeling scared, terrified; that your self is in danger of being destroyed

Resentment: feeling that the parent is being unreasonable and blaming you for something not under your control or for making a mistake; or feeling that the parent is taking unearned credit

These are strong and intense negative feelings, and there can be times when the feeling lingers for a long time. Moderating these feelings when they emerge so that they will be less intense and negative, and more under your conscious control, may be accomplished by doing one or more of the following:

- Ask yourself if your feeling could be a projection or part of a projection from your parent and remind yourself that you do not have to accept the feeling.

- Remind yourself that you can choose what to feel and then substitute a milder feeling, such as substituting apprehension for fear, unless fear is justifiable for the circumstances.

- Go to your place of peace for a few seconds and see if that moderates some of the intensity for the feeling.

- Quickly put your emotional insulation in place.

- Silently vow to yourself to do better next time, to not make the same mistake, to become less attached to the parent so that his emotions are not caught, and other such similar thoughts.

These are a few ways that you can choose your emotions. If the slings and arrows of put-downs, disparaging remarks, denigrations, and the like don't hit their mark, you will not be hurt, and the parent will not win.

LEARNING PROTECTIVE ACTIONS

You know that some form of an indirect or a direct attack will be mounted by your parent at some point, but you can be prepared to handle these.

It can be difficult to manage unexpected attacks or assaults on your essential self, because you were not prepared for them to happen. Chapter 2 presented an exercise that can serve as your emotional insulation, and you are encouraged to use this prior to interactions with your parent when possible, and even during interactions when you realize that your feelings are becoming intense. This is a good protective strategy. You can also review your list of positive attributes from exercise 9.1 to have a current reminder that you do have strengths and are in the process of developing more of these.

It is unfortunate that you are in a position where you cannot relax your vigilance when you are around your parent or when you are anticipating an interaction with him. While you may long for a different and more positive interaction, the reality may be that your desire will not be fulfilled. It is better to prepare for the worst and be pleasantly surprised when the worst does not happen than to not prepare and to be injured when it does.

The remainder of this chapter will describe and illustrate important considerations for choosing strategies and describe six additional strategies that you can use as protection; to help you manage attacks and assaults and conflict situations; and to help you protect others, such as your created family. The strategies addressed here will be deflect, distract, fog, neutral responses, distance, and drift. These are primarily passive actions, and if you tend to use more active strategies, these can seem foreign and difficult for you. Adjusting your response to meet varied situations and to cope with your aging self-absorbed parent can pay dividends for your emotional and psychological well-being, and you are encouraged to experiment with using some or all of these strategies.

Important Considerations for Choosing a Strategy

There are some important considerations to ponder when choosing a strategy. Among the most important ones are the context or situation, your parent's immediate goal and emotional state, your emotional state and vulnerability, the possible impact on others who may be present, and the importance, significance, or urgency of the issue or concern under discussion.

CONTEXT OR SITUATION

The context or situation refers to the physical setting, the presence or absence of others, and the reason for being in the interaction with your parent. The physical setting can be an important consideration for your choice because it may be in a place or context, such as a restaurant or other public venue, where it may be best for you to not engage with your parent; or it may be at what is supposed to be a celebration, such as a birthday party, a church service or gathering, or other similar settings.

PARENT GOAL AND EMOTIONAL STATE

Another consideration is your parent's goal and emotional state. It can be helpful to pause to try to assess what it is that your parent is trying to get: attention, admiration, power and control, or revenge. Also, try to gauge his emotional state and intensity when you are choosing how to respond. Could your parent be trying to provoke you, or is he expressing an intense and important personal concern?

YOUR EMOTIONAL VULNERABILITY AND CURRENT STATE

Central to a choice for a strategy is your emotional vulnerability and current state. You may not be able to use the suggested strategies when you are very vulnerable with a lot of emotional intensity. At those times, you are more likely to be injured by your parent, because you essentially have no protection. Assess your vulnerability and emotions before using any strategy, and if you are not in a place where you feel you can manage both yourself and your parent at the same time, you may find that it is best for you to protect your self by not being in your parent's presence. Do not engage with him when you are vulnerable and intense, as you are not able to use your defenses, such as emotional insulation, and this leaves you open to whatever he decides to do and to his projections. If, on the other hand, you are not as emotionally vulnerable or do not have a lot of emotional intensity, you may be able to manage both yourself and your parent and be more capable of choosing an appropriate strategy.

IMPACT ON OTHERS

You may also need to consider what the impact may be on others who are present, such as the other parent, children, family members, or guests and other nonfamily members. What you choose to do or say will affect others in varying ways, and you will want to stay mindful and considerate of others. Remember that no other person has the relationship that you have with your parent, including your other family members and especially people who interact and relate to your parent in other settings. You have seen the self-absorbed behaviors and attitudes for many years, but others have not; and most importantly, they have not had to encounter the same negativity directed toward them as that which you have encountered. Therefore, do not expect others to understand what you experience in interactions with your parent. Some may understand, and that is a plus, but your choice of action should not include the expectation that others who are present will understand what the parent is doing or your need to respond as you do.

IMPORTANCE AND URGENCY

The importance and urgency of the concern that is central to the interaction with your parent can be a guide for your choice of a strategy. There is one question to consider: Is it critical that this concern be addressed right now? You or your parent may think that it is urgent and important to engage at this moment, but it may well be that the concern is neither urgent nor important. You can use these four categories as a guide for your decision:

1. Important but not urgent. Time may be needed to allow all aspects of the concern to be reviewed, and the matter need not be addressed at this time.

2. Important and urgent. The matter is significant, and there is some urgency about it. However, unless someone's life is in danger, there is no need to address any matter when under duress. Important and urgent should be reserved for those times when immediate action is needed, such as when a life is in danger.

3. Urgent but not important. Matters in this category may be able to be addressed in another way, or else appropriate action can be taken without bringing anyone else into the matter, or the matter is urgent for only one of you.

4. Neither important nor urgent. Why bother about this at all?

You may want to take some time to reflect on past encounters with your parent; evaluate the importance and urgency of the topic, matter, or concern that was central; and finally determine which category those encounters best fit. You are likely to find more encounters that fit into the fourth category than in any other category. This is one reason why you may want to consider using some of the following strategies when you are under attack or assault by your self-absorbed parent.

Six Strategies for Protecting Your Self

No one strategy is helpful all of the time or more effective with a particular type of parent. You may also need to consider the effects of aging on your parent when selecting which strategy to use. It's difficult to describe what role aging will play for your particular parent, but you may want to keep this in mind when you make your selection of a strategy at a particular time.

DEFLECT

Deflection refers to doing or saying something that deflects the parent's attack or assault on you. The goal or objective can be to move the parent's attention to something that will be less hurtful to you. Deflection techniques include moving the focus to a minor or unrelated aspect of the topic, giving compliments, acting indifferent, and having a "Surely you don't mean me?" attitude.

An example of moving the focus can be seen in the situation when your parent is critical of you for something like not picking up his dry cleaning. To deflect, you could start talking about the increased cost of dry cleaning, or how the cleaners has not remodeled and really needs to do so, or how it is so difficult to get spots out of some fabrics. Asking a follow-up question about the new focus keeps the deflection going.

Complimenting the parent can also be a deflection when skillfully done. Using the same criticism as in the previous example, a complimenting response could be to tell the parent that he cares about his appearance and always looks nice. A follow-up comment or question would continue the deflection.

Acting indifferent can be effective but also has the potential to really irritate the parent, because it can be perceived by him as uncaring. What I recommend is that you act indifferent to the critical remarks (fake it if necessary) and respond only to the content. Continuing the scenario used in the previous two examples, acting indifferent would mean that your response would be only a commitment to get the cleaning to the parent on a particular day when you know that you can do that. Do not apologize, provide an explanation, or do anything similar. Simply say something like "I'll get it to you on Monday."

A "Surely you don't mean me?" attitude may be helpful as it can dilute and deflect the negative remarks from the parent, but it may be unwise to speak these thoughts out loud. When he is directing put-downs, denigrating comments, and other such uncomplimentary words at you, you can think, *Surely you don't mean me?* Since many of these parental remarks and comments tend to be exaggerations, or even not true of you at all, instead of explaining, protesting, or becoming defensive, you can tell yourself that what he is saying doesn't fit you, which will help you to ignore his negative comments.

DISTRACT

This strategy is almost the same as deflection, but it takes the attention to an entirely new topic. Think of what you do with children to keep them away from doing something dangerous or unwise, to prevent them from becoming or staying upset, or to get them away from an object. The same motives and actions will be something you may be able to use with your parent. Some examples of distraction are changing the topic, including another person in the conversation, and referring to another event.

Changing the topic. You are in a conversation with your parent, and he starts to make unfair comparisons of you with someone else, either saying or implying that you are inferior, lazy, unmotivated, or something else that is unflattering. Along with those remarks about you, he makes complimentary and admiring comments about someone else, such as a sibling. Your distracting response could be to introduce a new topic that is unrelated to what the parent is saying about you. Or you could expand on the compliments about the other person and note something else about that person that is exemplary, such as that the person plays a good game of golf, and then deflect the conversation to the new topic of golf.

Including another person. Using the same scenario, you can call the other person to join you and your parent. This distraction can cause the parent to change topics, as he now has to acknowledge the other person's presence and become sociable. Or you can redirect the conversation to the other person by bringing up other topics that will include the other person.

Referring to another event. Another example for distraction is for you to look around the environment where the discussion with your parent is taking place and note if there is an event there that you could call attention to, thereby providing a distraction. Another way to introduce an event as a distraction is to ask about a recent past event or an event in the future. The event does not have to be a major one. It's just to provide a distraction.

FOG

To get an idea of what fogging means, visualize a foggy day, a heavy downpour, or a blizzard where you cannot see anything clearly except maybe your immediate surroundings. You cannot see anything in the distance that you can usually see. Fogging techniques with your parent can include questioning, becoming present centered, and branching off.

Questioning. As an example of questioning, you can obscure the intent and meaning of the topic of concern that is leading to the parent blaming, criticizing, or denigrating you. Focus your responses on the topic and ask lots of questions about it, most of which do not provide relevant information but are still connected to the topic in some way. Don't try to overwhelm your parent with questions, as that can be perceived as an attack. Just continue to calmly ask meaningless questions.

Becoming present centered. This means that you act as if what the parent is complaining about caused you to remember to ask him about something important. The association does not have to relate in any way to what the parent was talking about. You can say something like "That reminds me. I've been meaning to ask you about [whatever]," or "You're reminding me that I need to talk with you about [something]." Be sure to have other topics in mind that could call for his memory or expertise or lead the parent to tell a story.

Branching off. To branch off means taking one part of what the parent is talking about and focusing on only that part. Use that part to go in a new direction so that the shift to another topic is gradual and subtle. Suppose the parent is blaming you for taking his car in to be fixed and something still isn't working right. He suggests that you deliberately took it someplace where the mechanics were incompetent. Branching off could be seen in you talking about the Better Business Bureau's rating procedures and how these don't provide enough information to make good choices.

NEUTRAL RESPONSES

Neutral responses are those that do not provide any clues that you are either accepting or rejecting what the parent says or means. You are not necessarily indifferent or uncaring; rather, you are not taking sides one way or the other about the matter. A neutral response can be disarming; as it does not provide a target or further ammunition for increasing the attack on you, it cannot be perceived as you being disrespectful or as an attack on him. Neutral responses include comments like "Really?" "How about that?" "I really need to think about this some more," and "Interesting."

"Really?" is a response that could be asking that the parent support or expand on what was said or how he feels. You don't have to follow this with a statement or a question; just let it hang between you and your parent.

"How about that?" is also neutral, as the receiver cannot tell what you are responding to—you may be referring to the topic, the content, or the feelings. Whatever the parent was saying, meaning, or intending did not receive a response from you that he could object to.

"I really need to think about this some more" conveys that you received what was said but are not clear on how it applies to you and want some time to reflect on it. You now have an option to reflect or not to reflect, but you do not have to do either at this time. If asked about it later, you can say something like "I'm still mulling it over. It's more complex than it appears to be on the surface," but do not explain anything.

"Interesting" is a response that may invite questions from your parent as to what part of his message provoked that response. "What's so interesting?" can be anticipated. Staying neutral in your response can be difficult, but here are some possible responses for those comebacks: "It's interesting that you bring this up now," "It's interesting that you have that perspective," or "It's interesting that this seems to be important for you at this time."

Do not get sucked into a debate or discussion with your parent, however he provokes you. Use another one of the neutral responses if the parent tries to continue the interaction.

DISTANCE

Distance can be helpful, as this removes you from being near the parent, which reduces opportunities for you to be susceptible to catching the parent's projections or emotions. As noted before, some nonverbal behaviors can be helpful under some circumstances. When you have to be near the parent, you can use some of these nonverbal distancing behaviors:

- Orient your body away from the parent. Turn slightly sideways.

- Slightly lean backward away from the parent.

- Refrain from direct eye contact.

- Stand three feet or more away from the parent.

- Stand in a position that helps you feel centered and grounded.

- When seated, hold something in your hands, cross your arms over your chest, cross your legs, or plant your feet on the floor as if you were preparing to move.

- Visualize your parent as being at the far end of a long tunnel where you can barely see or hear him.

You may also want to try these nonverbal body positions when you are talking with your parent over the phone, even if he cannot see you.

Other distancing techniques that can be helpful are to use e-mail for most communications with the parent and to not promptly respond to him. You can also read and send text messages sparingly, allowing some time to elapse before reading his response, and even allowing some more time before replying (unless, of course, there is an emergency).

Some people find that social media is helpful for staying updated with others. You can also use this as a way to keep the parent informed about what you think is important for the parent to know without being in physical contact. Choose what to share very carefully, and read the parent's responses judiciously and infrequently.

DRIFT

Drifting is both a cognitive technique and a behavior. When used as a cognitive technique, it allows you to get away from the parent in your head without verbalizing what you are thinking. You could drift away by daydreaming about an ideal vacation, winning the lottery and how you would spend some of the money, what you would do if you were asked to participate in your favorite TV show or be in a movie, planning an event, or anything. Drifting to something else prevents you from catching your parent's projected feelings, having your negative feelings triggered, or being tempted to buy into your parent's perception of you. You can still hear the words, but you are primarily in your own world for that period of time.

Another way to drift is to focus on something in the environment and carefully examine it. Suppose you are in a living or family room, and there is a sofa with small throw pillows. You can look at a pillow and notice its size, shape, colors, and the texture of the fabric, mentally trace the design on it, and picture the softness within—in other words, mentally explore everything you see about the pillow. Another example could be to concentrate on the interplay of light, shadow, and darkness in the space where you are and notice how that interplay makes subtle changes as you pay attention to it. If you are out of doors, there are many opportunities to drift.

If you decide that drifting is an option you can use, you will also want to be judicious when using it and not employ it all the time when interacting with your parent. And it may be best if you do not use it in interactions with others with whom you have an important relationship. Drifting should be used sparingly.

SUMMARY

There are many suggested strategies and techniques presented in previous chapters to help you cope with the negative behaviors and attitudes of your self-absorbed parent, and those can also serve to protect your self from being wounded by him. This chapter extended the previous suggestions by providing descriptions of techniques that are protective of you when you are in interactions with the parent, as well as some possible growth and development strategies for building and fortifying your inner self. It is growing and developing that will bring you the most relief and satisfaction. Becoming the person you want to be promotes healthy separation and individuation from your parent and allows you to foster a strong, resilient inner self that can form and maintain enduring, satisfying, and meaningful relationships. You can better demonstrate empathy and caring for others and reduce or eliminate possible self-absorbed behaviors and attitudes that you cannot see.

Chapter 10 provides some specific steps that you can take to help protect others, such as your children, spouse, partner, and other such important people in your life, from the negative behaviors and attitudes of your self-absorbed parent. These are the people who mean the most to you, who may not understand how your parent affects them, and who have few if any resources to help them cope.

CHAPTER 10

Protecting Others

It is important to remember the possible effects of aging on your parent as presented in chapter 1, because some aging effects can explain why the parent's self-absorbed behaviors and attitudes are becoming worse. Understanding these effects can also help set the framework for beginning to develop strategies to protect your loved ones, especially your created family. Some additional aging effects can be the following:

- May be retired and now wants to spend more time with you and the grandchildren

- At loose ends: lack of social connections, meaningful work, attention, or other resources

- More demanding and needy of your time and patience

- Has not relinquished the parental role and still acts and reacts as if you were a child

- Appeals to or preys on your sympathy, pity, and good nature and will do the same with your family

You are the buffer and protection for your created family to help prevent them from experiencing the injuries to the essential self, negative feelings and thoughts about oneself, and other distress that you encountered with your self-absorbed parent.

WHY IT CAN BE DIFFICULT TO EXPLAIN TO OTHERS

The difficulties with trying to explain your parent's behaviors and attitudes and the effects of these on you result from the abstract nature of many of the self-absorbed behaviors and attitudes, as these have to be inferred. For example, envy and inner emptiness are not readily visible in overt behaviors but have to be inferred from behaviors and outcomes over time. Another problem arises from the reluctance and inadvisability of trying to characterize someone from one event or incident, as that can be unfair. In short, to characterize someone as self-absorbed—even your parent, who says and does distressing things—requires that she exhibit several of the self-absorbed behaviors and attitudes and that she does so rather consistently.

An additional complication can be the personality and experiences of others in your family that permit them to perceive your parent's behaviors and attitudes in a different way than you do. It can be helpful for you to remember that you have years of experiences with that parent, and your created family does not. Since everyone's experience of your self-absorbed parent differs, your family may not be able to understand what you describe as your experiences, and you need to be patient with them. What others can see are your reactions, and they may or may not understand why you react as you do. Your parent has a different relationship with your family members, and it is helpful to try to remember this as you try to describe what that parent can say and do that produces distress for you and may do the same for them. The remainder of this chapter focuses on your personal preparation to be a protector, on strategic planning, and on protection techniques.

YOUR PERSONAL PREPARATION

Before beginning to help anyone else, you first have to do some personal preparation. You cannot afford to be totally spontaneous and react to incidents as they appear. You must anticipate events, choose what to do or say as an intervention, recognize some of your parent's motives for the distressing behaviors and attitudes, and communicate and prepare your family members in accord with their age and abilities. It is best that you not wait until a family member has been distressed or injured to prepare to protect, but it's also never too late to do so. Take the following under consideration:

- Expect your parent's self-absorbed behaviors and attitudes to intensify with age, especially those behaviors and attitudes that define the type, such as complaining for the clingy type.

- Recognize and accept that your family will take their cues from you and that how you react and act models behavior for them and can determine their emotional reactions.

- When a distressing event happens to a family member, mentally plan a thirty-second freak-out at a distant time and place. Don't freak out in the presence of either the parent or your family.

Additional personal preparation includes strategic planning based on your prior experiences and reflection about your parent.

STRATEGIC PLANNING

There will be less distress and turmoil if you can do some planning in advance of family interactions where your self-absorbed parent will be present. Doing so allows you an opportunity to reflect and plan when you are less emotionally intense and do not need to be alert to possible attacks or assaults. You will also be able to institute some protective strategies for your family. This planning process involves anticipating what the self-absorbed parent is likely to say and do that could be distressing for one or more of your family members, assessing the probably negative emotional intensity which those actions could produce, and reflecting about possible preinteraction and interaction interventions. Sounds a bit complicated, and it is; however, explanations are provided, and I encourage you to try some of these strategies.

Anticipating what your self-absorbed parent is likely to say and do that could produce distress is based on your prior experiences with that parent and your understanding of the members of your created family.

For example, if your parent tries to disguise her denigrating remarks and comments by calling those teasing, then you can anticipate that the parent is likely to do the same to members of your created family. The following exercise can help you get started on anticipating what your created family may encounter in interactions with your self-absorbed parent.

Exercise 10.1: Anticipating the Self-Absorbed Parent

Materials: Several sheets of paper and a pen or pencil for writing, or a tablet or computer

Procedure:

1. Find a place to work where you will not be interrupted or distracted.

2. Make a list of numbers from 1 to 20 for each item on the scale.

Parental Behavior/Attitude Scale

Rate the extent to which you can expect your parent to exhibit each of the following behaviors or attitudes:

1—Never or almost never

2—Seldom; not often, but it does occur

3—Often, sometimes unexpectedly

4—Very often, considerably

5—Always or almost always; extensively

- Teases

- Uses taunting comments

- Uses sarcasm

- Some comments are put-downs

- Makes demands on others

- Gives orders and expects compliance

- Complains

- Makes snarky comments or remarks

- Puts negative labels on others

- Mocks others' values and concerns

- Makes fun of others (appearance, agility, clothing, and so on)

- Makes snide comments that suggest that others are inferior

- Is openly critical of others

- Blames others, does not accept blame

- Provides compliments that are disguised insults

- Tries to arouse guilt

- Shows contempt for others

- Fails to show gratitude or be appreciative

- Lacks empathy

- Is inclined to yell at others

3. Next, list the behaviors or attitudes that you rated as 4 and 5 on a sheet of paper, leaving some space between them to write more information. For each item, write a description of the act that the parent uses that fits the term. For example, if you rated teasing as 5, you could describe the act as: teasing you about a crush you had on someone, teasing you about the color of your hair, or teasing you for losing your hair. Be as specific as possible when describing the parent's actions for the behavior or attitude.

4. If you feel that the actions rated as 3 might be very hurtful for one or more members of your created family, repeat step 3 for these. You now have a list of negative behaviors and attitudes that you can

expect to happen. This list can help you focus your development of protective strategies for your family.

The second part of the exercise focuses on the emotional intensity the parent's actions aroused for you or for each of your family members.

5. Return to the original list of twenty behaviors and attitudes, draw a table with a column for each of your family members; put the names of the family members at the top of the columns, and record a probable emotional intensity reaction rating for each item in the list for each family member using the following scale:

    1—Not distressed

    2—Bothered, but not necessarily distressed

    3—Distressed

    4—Very distressed

    5—Extremely distressed

Example:

Parent	Your Distress	Spouse/Partner Distress	Child 1 Distress	Child 2 Distress
Teasing	4	2	5	4

6. After rating emotional intensity reactions for each family member, make a list of the behaviors and attitudes that could produce the emotional intensity or distress rated as 3, 4, or 5 for every family member.

Example:

Spouse/partner: put-downs, mocking, blame

Child 1: teasing, taunting, yelling

Child 2: teasing, taunting, criticism

This last list provides you with information about when to intervene for each family member to protect that family member. You will also know which of your parent's actions are distressful for everyone and those that may be distressful only to you.

Here are five possible actions or attitudes that could be distressful and some examples for interventions or protections. You may want to write down other thoughts and ideas that occur to you as you read this. Additional examples and suggestions are discussed later in this chapter.

Action	Interventions
Sarcasm	Take what is said at face value and respond in a thoughtful, calm manner; laugh and change the topic; ignore it.
Contempt	If possible, smile and say that there are varying perspectives and that is a good thing; do not retaliate in kind; say the equivalent of "Oh, well."
Yelling	Say, "Is it possible to use an inside voice?" If your child is present, send him or her to get something for you to remove the child from the yelling; ask the parent what's producing the yelling; get family members out of the parent's presence; take a bathroom break.
Complaints	Sympathize but do not try to fix it; give a neutral response; do not explain or become defensive if the parent's complaint is about you.
Teasing	Do not respond; shrug your shoulders; change the topic, ask an unrelated question; do not show your real feelings; do not protest.

These are also suggestions that your family members can use. There may also be behaviors or attitudes that your parent uses that are not listed in the rating scale, and you are encouraged to use the same process described here to produce some possible interventions or protective strategies for you and for your family.

Other Protective Principles and Strategies

Here are four principles that can be helpful for you to adopt as part of your protective strategies. You may be able to think of one or two additional ones.

1. The emotional and psychological welfare of your created family is a first, or most significant, priority.

2. Your aging self-absorbed parent merits some consideration and respect, no matter how you feel about her.

3. You must maintain your integrity and abide by your core values, and your actions will reflect these.

4. A goal is to act so as to teach others how to manage and thrive under these conditions and thereby reinforce your determination to do so yourself.

When you feel flustered or overwhelmed, you can remind yourself about these principles and they will guide you to choose an action or strategy. Keeping these principles in mind, let's move on to categories of protective strategies.

PROTECTIVE STRATEGIES

Even when you have reason to believe that your self-absorbed parent will behave in a certain way, you may not communicate enough specifics to your family so that they understand, and you may not teach them how to cope with your parent. This section is intended to provide you with suggestions and ideas that you can use, and to get you started on developing some that are unique to you and your situation.

Preparing Family Members

There are three major considerations for preparing family members: the ages of your family members, explicit family rules and priorities, and implicit family rules and priorities.

Most families have members who vary in age, and your family is probably no different. It can be important for you to know that how old your family members are will play a role in what and how you communicate, what they can expect from your self-absorbed parent, how they can respond, and, most importantly, what they can expect you to do and say to protect them. It would be very unusual for you to have purposefully communicated all of this prior to reading this book, which is not to say that you have not tried to prepare them in the past. You may have tried to prepare them but not in the manner that follows, which is purposeful, specific, and goal directed.

Your family's explicit rules and priorities may be very well articulated and followed, but let's take a little time to reflect on what your rules and priorities are.

Exercise 10.2:   Explicit Family Rules

Materials: A sheet of paper and a pen or pencil for writing, or a digital device for recording

Procedure: Find a place to work where you will not be interrupted or distracted. Make a list of your family's explicit rules. These are the expectations that guide behavior and are verbalized. Think of what you and your spouse or partner explicitly say to your children, such as the following:

"Brush your teeth before bedtime."

"Say please and thank you."

"Do not call adults by their first names. Address adults as Mr., Mrs., Ms., or Miss."

"Show consideration and appreciation for each other."

"Ask permission to borrow someone's possessions."

Compile a list of your explicit set of family rules.

This exercise can also help increase your awareness of where you and your family are acting on some implicit family rules that may need to be explicitly stated when preparing your family for encounters with your self-absorbed parent.

Implicit family rules are expectations for behavior that are not openly or verbally communicated and are open to interpretation, or may not be fully understood by all. Some of these may be yours alone, and some can be shared. But almost always, these are ambiguous and subject to being misunderstood by one or more family members, were not set collaboratively, and may be more influential and powerful than explicit rules. It can be very helpful if many of these are known and articulated to family members. You may want to solicit input from your family members on what they perceive to be implicit family rules. Complete the following exercise alone first. After doing so, you could involve other family members either separately or in a group.

Exercise 10.3: Implicit Family Rules

Materials: A sheet of paper and a pen or pencil for writing, or a digital device for recording

Procedure:

1. Find a place to work with a suitable writing surface and where you will not be interrupted or distracted.

2. Compile a list of your implicit family rules: the expectations you have for behaviors that are not openly and explicitly stated. These may be assumed to be known by all so that any violations are perceived as being willful and may produce annoyance for you; they are reflective of your deeply held values. Examples could include the following:

   Always come to a family member's defense.

Do not express disagreement openly.

Be neat and clean.

Be grateful.

Parents protect children.

Children's [or parents'] needs have priority.

3. Once you have created your list, review it and note which of these implicit rules may need to be more explicit to help prepare and protect your family.

Another helpful step would be to solicit input from your spouse or partner and your children. Note what rules they see as implicit and ask if there are other family rules that could be helpful or need to become more explicit.

Preparation Strategies

Engaging in exercises 10.2 and 10.3 provides a basis for the following preparation strategies:

- ■ Basic expectations for family members' behavior with the self-absorbed parent

- ■ Reliance on family rules as priorities

- ■ What you can and will do if family members are distressed

- ■ How family members can manage their feelings

I suggest that you discuss these with your family members as appropriate, given their ages and other characteristics, and do so prior to their encounters with your self-absorbed parent.

BASIC EXPECTATIONS

Basic expectations for your family members' behavior can simply be civility and courtesy, such as that which is extended to everyone, including strangers. You may need to explicitly state that you do not expect your family members to accept or to give the self-absorbed parent affection or affectionate gestures if they do not want to do so. Make it clear that your expectation is that any affectionate acts by them are their choice, and you neither demand nor expect such from them toward your parent. However, you must also make it clear that you do expect them to exhibit good manners.

RELYING ON FAMILY RULES

Most helpful for your family will be the knowledge that you will support their reliance on your family rules as priorities for behavior and reactions. If these rules have been established and communicated similarly to what is suggested in exercises 10.2 and 10.3, there will be little doubt or confusion about what these are and that these are the guides your family can use when there may be conflicting demands, ambiguity, and uncertainty produced by interactions with your self-absorbed parent. For example, if the self-absorbed parent admonished your spouse or child for disagreeing with her about something, you could support that family member by remarking that your family rules allow for expressing differences of opinion in a respectful way (assuming this is one of your family's rules). Knowing that family rules are a priority can give family members confidence that you will approve of their choices of behavior or actions in response to your self-absorbed parent.

Your family will have less lingering distress aroused by interactions with your self-absorbed parent if you can explicitly state that you want and expect family members to immediately tell you whenever something said or done by the self-absorbed parent is distressing for them. Being notified immediately gives you a chance to do the following:

1. Affirm your relationship with the family member.

2. Empathize with the family member's reactions. (By far, this will be the most helpful action you can take. You do not have to agree; just understand.)

3. Remind your family member that your self-absorbed parent may initiate the distress but that the family member is well prepared to manage that distress.

4. When a family member is criticized, you can find the strength that could be embedded in a criticism. Doing so can be a means of support and encouragement for the family member (exercise 10.4 guides you in this process).

It is important for your family relationships that you help family members manage their distress when your self-absorbed parent does any of the behaviors in exercise 10.1 or other behaviors that produce distress. Reassurance about your relationship and its importance to you, providing empathic responses, reaffirming your confidence in your family member's ability to manage the distress, and finding a strength in the criticism can do much to mediate the negative effects of the self-absorbed parent on family members. The next exercise shows how to look for hidden resources in criticism, and how you can find these in yourself, as a guide to working with any of your family members to help them find their embedded strengths in themselves.

Exercise 10.4:   Hidden Resources

Materials: One or more sheets of paper and a pen or pencil, or a suitable digital device

Procedure:

1. Find a place to work where you will not be interrupted or disturbed. Take one sheet of paper and draw a line down the page vertically so that you have two columns.

2. Label column 1 "Criticism/Fault" and column 2 "Strength."

3. In column 1, list the behaviors for which you are or were criticized or that you think of as faults. You do not have to agree with the criticisms, but list all criticisms that you have received, especially those delivered by your self-absorbed parent and those received from others two or more times.

4. Now find or think of a possible strength that the criticized behavior or fault may be concealing. Some examples follow:

Criticism/Fault	Strength
Lazy	Conserving resources, finding a more efficient and effective way to accomplish the task, enjoying the present
Daydreaming	Using imagination, planning, visualizing solutions, organizing thoughts

You can use the same process to find a strength hidden in the critical remarks of your self-absorbed parent toward one of your family members. Focusing on strengths does not have to minimize or deny the criticism, but it does help to show the receiver that whatever is being criticized is not all bad or shameful. Focusing on a strength can encourage the receiver to capitalize on the strength, which is much more helpful than trying to remediate a deficiency, especially one that may have some shame connected to it.

YOUR INTERVENTIONS

You may also want to directly state to your family that you will intervene if they signal they are in distress. One recommendation presented in more detail later on in this chapter is that you remain alert so as to be aware when an interaction with your self-absorbed parent seems to be producing distress for a family member, and you can tell family members that you will be monitoring interactions so that you can quickly come to their rescue if needed.

Explain that you will be ready to do something similar to the following:

- Deflect the parent's attention.

- Distract the parent by introducing another topic.

- Find an excuse to remove your family member from the interaction (take a walk, play a game, and so on).

- Use fogging, such as paying the parent a compliment and thereby making her the center of attention.

- Remind all that family rules are priorities.

One intervention that may be difficult to do is to tell your parent, "Do. Not. Do. That." in a strong, decisive manner. You do not have to yell, raise your voice, or show anger or other signs of distress. You can say it calmly and in a manner that conveys your meaning and intent that the parent should immediately cease the action. This intervention should be reserved for important, urgent, and dire circumstances. Examples of such circumstances would be unwelcomed physical contact, hitting, restraining acts, touching body parts such as a breast or rear end, telling off-color jokes that produce discomfort or that are inappropriate for some people who are present, recounting erotic stories, and other similar acts.

In addition to telling the parent to cease, you can leave her presence, remove your family members, and not rush to explain or overly explain your rationale for what you said. This intervention is difficult because it is a confrontation and, as noted earlier in the book, confrontations usually do not work with self-absorbed people. It may be best to refrain from using confrontation with your parent. Nevertheless, it is proposed here that you consider doing so to protect your family. But you must also be prepared to suffer the consequences, such as the parent becoming angry with you. The circumstances may be such that this strategy is needed, but hopefully, such circumstances are rare and other more moderate interventions will suffice. The important point in all of this is that your family members know that you are willing and prepared to protect them.

MANAGING THEIR FEELINGS

Your family members can help themselves by learning some techniques to manage distress and other such feelings aroused in interactions with your self-absorbed parent. Following is a process that can be helpful to teach them and for you to use.

1. Notice what you are feeling at the time when you are interacting.

2. Give the feeling an intensity rating from 1 (for no distress with little or no intensity) to 10 (for extreme distress with very high intensity).

3. If your rating of your feeling is 5 or higher, proceed to the next steps. If it is less than 5, you may be managing well on your own.

4. Take a deep breath and try to concentrate on your breathing to make it deep and even. You are most relaxed when your breath is deep and even.

5. Try to breathe from your diaphragm, which is just above your stomach. If you notice that you have quick short breaths, consciously try to breathe deeper.

6. Go to your head and think about your breathing. Do not stay completely focused on your feelings and their intensity. You can also try one or more of the following at this point: notice something else in the environment; concentrate on your breath and not on what is being said or done that produced your distress; become aware of other bodily sensations, such as the location of muscle tension, and try to relax those muscles by alternately tightening and relaxing them; look around for the parent (you) to come to your rescue; think about something beautiful or pleasant; recall a humorous event, but do not laugh out loud, just smile inwardly; imagine the offending person on a cloud drifting away from you or visualize a similar image.

These suggestions for managing feelings are for the immediate situation and will allow the person experiencing the feelings to not become so emotionally intense. This process can help the person decide to not act out and can also serve to block an unconscious acceptance of projections from your self-absorbed parent. You may also want to teach your family members the technique of emotional insulation described in exercise 2.7.

Social Media

Social media are used for a variety of reasons and can be very helpful for some situations. However, the use of social media can be contraindicated when you have a self-absorbed aging parent. Your family may physically interact with that parent, even if they do so infrequently, and may need some guidance about material disclosed on social media so as not to provide that parent with ammunition she can use to attack them, or to criticize, blame, denigrate, or the like. This also applies to you, not just to your family members.

Even if you do not use social media to inform or to connect with your self-absorbed parent, you must not assume that others whom you do allow on your site will not pass on the information you post. Your parent may not use social media or even a computer, but others do, and they may not realize the impact on you and your family members when they pass on information you posted that you did not intend for your parent to have. It's easy to post something that your self-absorbed parent can use against you or against your family.

There are three primary points to govern your and your family's use of social media: monitoring, selecting, and not venting.

MONITORING

Monitor what you and your family members post when possible so that you can be prepared for what your parent may try to use that will produce injury or distress. Being mentally and emotionally prepared means that you are well on your way to being able to prevent distress and protect family members.

SELECTING

Selecting what to post can be tricky. After all, the reason to post is to inform and to maintain connections. The guiding principle for selection is to always keep in mind how the posting may have the potential to hurt, denigrate, or be used in unintended ways against you and your family. Make it a practice to try to not post anything that is unflattering to you or a family member. While the posting may be humorous or cute, your thoughts should be about your self-absorbed parent's misuse of it to tease, taunt, criticize, and the like.

AVOID VENTING

Some people use social media to make known some of their concerns, the adversity in their lives, and other such topics. It can be best to not do this, as once again you may be providing your self-absorbed parent with material that she can use to your detriment. This suggestion also applies to these kinds of disclosures to others, who may intentionally or unintentionally reveal the information to your parent.

A Final Suggestion

I don't know if you have ever been around hovering parents who are always somewhere in the vicinity of their child or children, or if you are this kind of parent yourself, but hovering is a strategy you could adopt when your family has to be in the presence of and interact with your parent. This can be especially effective if you have concerns or reason to expect that your parent will do or say things to your family that could produce hurt and other intense emotions.

There are some constraints that can result when you hover: you cannot relax, you do not get to interact very much with others who are present, and you may be sending a signal of your mistrust of your parent. Hovering demands that you remain vigilant, alert, poised to intervene; that you stay close to the child or spouse or partner, and are constantly on edge. It's almost impossible to relax under those conditions. The payoff, however, can be less emotional intensity and less need to soothe hurt feelings after you get home or even during the visit. Another possible positive is that there will be less time and opportunity for your negative feelings to become aroused, as you are too busy taking care of others to be as open and concerned about yourself. Being the protector can be a shield for you.

Hovering over your family decreases the time you have available for interactions with others who may be with you, and this may or may not be a good thing for you. If you enjoy or want to converse with others who are present, hovering will vastly limit these opportunities. If, however, those interactions are not rewarding or enjoyable, then not having the time to interact is another positive.

The most sensitive constraint is that your hovering could be taken by your parent as a signal that you mistrust her with your family members. While this may be absolutely accurate on your parent's part, it could also arouse the parent's anger, which can then be directed toward you. Some self-absorbed parents would pick up the signal while others may completely miss it. You need to be prepared to cope if your parent picks up on the mistrust and then challenges you about it. If challenged, you can do the following:

- Do not confirm or deny the charge.

- Do not protest or say that you do trust her.

- Smile and give a neutral response.

- Use the strategies discussed in chapter 8.

- Say something like "I like to be around [the family member's name]."

Do not let your parent bully you into relaxing your hovering. You may want to back off a little, but do not abandon your family members to the actions of your parent.

SUMMARY

I hope that this chapter gave you some ideas and triggered new ideas and thoughts about protective strategies you can use for your family when they have to interact with your self-absorbed parent. Neither you nor they have to suffer emotional and psychological distress because of the actions of your self-absorbed parent. Nor are you helpless to come to their assistance through preparation and active interventions. It may not be possible for you or anyone else to be able to prevent your family members from encountering some distress, but using these strategies should decrease how often this happens and the negative effects on your family members.

CHAPTER 11

Winning and Thriving

You can succeed in shedding much of the baggage you may be carrying as a result of living with your self-absorbed parent during your formative years and beyond. Some of this baggage can be never feeling that you are good enough; considerable self-doubt; diminished self-esteem; constantly seeking to please others even at your own expense; fear of intimacy (a siege response); overreacting to implied or real criticism; an inability to be pleased, appreciative, or grateful; being on edge most or all of the time; and easily feeling shamed.

What's in your baggage that can be shed? While it may not be possible to shed some of the negatives, you can get rid of some or much of them. This is a major step toward thriving. You are probably on your way through your own efforts and, if you can implement some of the suggestions in this book, you can journey even further toward a goal to thrive.

WHAT YOU CAN DO TO ACHIEVE SUCCESS AND THRIVE

There are seven categories of actions you can take, attitudes that you can change, and other adjustments that will encourage and support you achieving success and will foster thriving. While letting go of the negatives can be positive in and of itself, this is more likely to happen when you build and fortify the positive aspects of your self so that you are more like the person you want to be. Wishing to be more confident with your self-absorbed parent, for example, does not make you more self-confident. However, you can become more confident when you work to accept yourself as you are, with strengths and weaknesses; are able to manage and contain the intense and negative emotions that can be aroused by your parent's words, actions, and attitudes; and can help protect your family and show them how to cope with your self-absorbed parent. There are probably other benchmarks that signal progress and success for having more confidence. Whatever it is that will make you feel successful can be worked on and achieved if you can do the following:

- Focus on your goals

- Visualize success

- Practice positive self-care

- Reach out to others

- Work to recognize and achieve positives

- Handle adversity

- Achieve balance

Each category will help trigger your thoughts about a set of specific actions for you to consider and decide if any of these fit you or your situation. You are also encouraged to think of other possible actions you can take to achieve success and to thrive.

Focus on Your Goals

Why have goals to be successful and thrive? Because having and achieving goals are major cornerstones in the *positive revenge* of being successful and thriving. Negative revenge does no one any good, and the few minutes of pleasure that it can bring don't translate into compensation for the offenses. Yes, the recipient may be discomforted, but you don't gain anything. Positive revenge is when you gain something that enriches you in spite of what the others did or said that was intended to show themselves as being superior and to demoralize you. It can really grate on them that you did not let their negativity thwart you from achieving your goals and becoming successful. Spend your energy on enriching your goals for yourself rather than on trying to find ways to make others regret the negative acts and comments they made to you. This will be a better use of your time and energy and produce positive results for you; at the same time, you will have your revenge.

Succeeding and thriving will take work. Getting rid of old baggage that is negatively affecting your progress needs more than a decision by you to do so and willpower. The old baggage can be so heavy and deeply rooted that it will not be easy to dislodge. In addition, you can unconsciously defend yourself from awareness and understanding about the baggage, and this is why working with a competent therapist can assist you with getting rid of it.

The other side to succeeding and thriving includes the active things you can do to assist your growth and development toward becoming the person you want to be. The process begins with you describing the realistic ideal self that you want. Notice that realistic and ideal are not separate here, as both are possibilities. An example of a goal would be freedom from worry, but a more realistic goal could be an ability to manage adversity. It is realistic to expect to have adversity that produces worries, but you don't have to stay mired in worry, as you can be confident that you will be able to manage adversity. Complete the following exercise to get started on defining your unique perception of what success and thriving means for you.

Exercise 11.1: Realistic or Fantasy

Materials: Several sheets of paper and a pen or pencil, or a suitable digital device

Procedure:

1. Find a place to work that has a suitable writing surface and is free from distractions and interruptions.

2. Reflect a few minutes on what you desire to be or to have happen that defines success and thriving for you. As you identify these

characteristics or actions, write them in list form. Your list could include such items as "happy," "free of self-doubt," "respect," "lack of intense negative emotions," and "feeling in control of self and of how others treat me." Try to list five to ten items.

3. Review your list and label each item as realistic or as fantasy. Realistic means that there is a good chance that you can attain this. Fantasy means that the item would be nice to get or to have, but the world doesn't work that way, and you are unlikely to get it. For example, freedom from worry is a fantasy, but being able to cope and manage adversity is realistic.

4. Next take each item on your list that you labeled realistic and write that item at the top of a separate page. Using the list in step 2 as an example, let's say that you designated happy and respect as realistic. You would then write "happy" at the top of one page and "respect" at the top of another page.

5. The next task is to define and describe what acts, feelings, situations, and the like are reflective of these realistic goals. Think about what needs to occur for you to feel that you attained that goal. For example, what constitutes happy for you? Write it down under the word "happy." Don't try to edit or evaluate your thoughts at this point; just write down everything that comes to mind as you contemplate being happy. Do the same for each of your realistic outcomes.

6. After you develop these lists for each goal, rate each item on the new lists as realistic (under your control) or fantasy (not under your control). Then make a new list on each page of the realistic items.

7. Review the new lists of realistic possibilities, imagine attaining these, and rate how satisfying it would be for you to experience these on a scale of 1 (not satisfying) to 5 (extremely satisfying). Items rated 4 and 5 are your benchmarks for achieving success and thriving.

8. Finally, reframe or redirect your thoughts and energies about the items you designated as fantasy on any of the lists. Begin by taking new sheets of paper and listing these items separately. Using the list provided in step 2 as an example, the new sheets would have "free

of self-doubt," "lack of intense negative emotions," and "feeling in control of self and of how others treat me" as the labels. Reflect on each of these items and try to think of what you can do that would be more realistic but is still related to what you want. For example, "freedom from worry" could be reframed as "having confidence that I can cope with adversity." Redirecting could be that you would increase your coping skills.

Reframing or redirecting fantasy goals guides your thoughts and energies into thinking of what you can do that is achievable and realistic. You now have two lists you created that can assist you in choosing actions that are encouraging and supportive.

Visualize Success

Winners can visualize being successful. They don't visualize failure, even though that is a possibility. This visualization is not a fantasy, such as what you can have about winning a huge lottery jackpot. This sort of visualization imagines the steps needed to succeed, what needs to be done at each step, barriers that may or do exist and how these can be managed or overcome, and effective use of your internal and external resources. It's called visualization because the process is mental. The images are produced by you and are used to show you unfolding events and possibilities.

Success for coping with your aging self-absorbed parent who will not change or improve is not an all-or-nothing situation; it is very much an individual determination. By that, I mean that neither I nor anyone else can define success for you or know when you've reached it. This is yours alone to determine, and what this chapter presents is only a guide with some examples to start your thinking, your visualizations, and your personal definitions for success. If you completed exercise 11.1, you now have a goal or goals, some sense of benchmarks to identify progress, and maybe even some objectives to guide your work.

Visualization of success requires that the outcome or goal be realistic and capable of being accomplished. It also calls for you to have a

realistic perception of your capabilities, determination, and resourceful-
ness. Notice that all of this is about you, and whatever you visualize
needs to be mainly or totally under your control. Take a moment now
to quickly think about what you would term *success* in coping with your
parent. Does your definition of success reflect any of the following?

- Your parent recognizing and appreciating your worth

- Being able to show your parent that he is wrong or inadequate

- A sense of satisfaction for you at the parent's failure or
  discomfort

- Taking attention and/or admiration away from the parent

- Getting an upper hand in a conflict or argument with the
  parent

- Becoming more powerful than your parent

- Others perceiving you as superior to your parent in an important way

If your idea of success reflects any of these or something along
similar lines, then I encourage you to try to revise your vision for success
to be more about enhancing your self and not about besting your parent.
Think about having a personal definition of success that includes some
or all of the following:

- Meaning and purpose in your life

- Strong, satisfying, and enduring personal relationships

- Happiness and serenity in most parts of your life

- The inclusion of hope, beauty, wonder, and zest in your everyday life

- A capacity to be empathic

- An appropriate sense of humor

- A fighting spirit

- Managing emotions so that they are constructive

- A deeper and more positive understanding of yourself

- Self-confidence, self-efficacy, and realistic self-esteem

You will find that it is infinitely more satisfying and rewarding to foster your self-development, which can lead to better relationships and a stronger sense of who you are as a separate and distinct individual, and as someone who is appreciative and kind to self and to others. This can produce a self that is able to manage the negativity produced from and by your self-absorbed parent, protect your family, and still be able to be a respectful adult to your parent in spite of what he does or says that is intended to criticize, demean, or dismiss you.

Practice Positive Self-Care

Self-care is very different from self-absorption. Self-absorption is a focus on oneself either exclusively or almost so in behaviors, attitudes, words, and deeds. The self-absorbed person may be aware of some of his self-focus that comes through to others, especially those people who must interact with him on a regular basis, such as family members. But many are not aware, and many more don't care. This book has described much about the self-absorbed parent who is aging, is unlikely to change, does not show empathy, and wants to maintain control over others. However, this section is focused on you, not your parent.

Self-care refers to the active steps you take to ensure health, positive outcomes, and continued growth and development in all aspects of your life: cognitive or mental, relational, emotional, creative, inspirational, and physical. Self-care does not mean or imply self-absorption, but it does emphasize a strong and healthy inner psychological self that permits you to have a rich and rewarding life that includes meaningful relationships and an awareness and appreciation for the positives in your life. Following are a few examples for each category:

Cognitive. Engage in activities that use the brain, such as problem-solving, decision making, event planning, card and other such games, reading, learning, and the like.

Relational. Working to maintain enduring and satisfying relationships, care and consideration for others you care about, and being empathic.

Emotional. Feeling and expressing a variety of emotions, especially positive ones; increased awareness of levels of emotions; managing and containing negative emotions; ability to feel but not become mired in negative emotions.

Creative. Try new and novel things that enhance your life; try to perceive everyday activities, events, and things from varying perspectives; seek new ways; use old things in new ways; write, draw, sculpt, dance, sing.

Inspirational. Appreciate beauty and wonder; maintain meaning and purpose for your life; perform altruistic acts; be kind; encourage your fighting spirit; celebrate your growth and development; work through challenges; connect to the universe.

Physical. Practice good health habits; eat healthy; exercise; get sufficient sleep; get regular medical and dental checkups.

Exercise 11.2:   Self-Care

Materials: Sheets of paper and a pen or pencil, or an appropriate digital device

Procedure:

1. Find a place to write where you will be free from distractions and interruptions. Make a list of the self-care categories—cognitive, relational, emotional, creative, inspirational, and physical—with sufficient space between the categories to write more material. Under each category, list the activities you regularly engage in for that category. Title this page "My Current Self-Care."

2. Make another list of the same categories, and under each category, list the activities that would enhance this category that you want to or could adopt. For example, under "physical," you may want to

write "eat less empty-calorie food," "eat more fruit," and "exercise more." Try to have two or more activities for each category. Title this list "My Self-Care Enhancements."

3. After completing step 2, return to that list and give each item a rating.

5—Very likely to follow through with this

4—Likely to follow through with this

3—Desirable, but may be difficult to do on a regular basis

2—May be easily dissuaded from following through on this

1—Unlikely to follow through

4. Use another sheet of paper to list all of the activities you rated 4 or 5, and give each a start date to begin to work on it. This is your action plan.

You can further develop your action plan by noting under each item the constraints or barriers you think you will encounter and steps you can take to overcome these. Another step is to set a checkup date for a review of your progress.

Keep this action plan and review the items periodically; celebrate your progress toward attaining these, and add new ones when any emerge.

Reach Out to Others

The connections you make to others can be some of the most rewarding parts of your life, and you are encouraged to work to strengthen and maintain the ones that mean the most to you. In addition, you are encouraged to reach out to others who are in need, in distress, and the like, and give of yourself to help them without any expectation of reciprocity. This is what is meant by altruism, and it is very different from doing favors for others who are supposed to do favors for you in return. Altruism is a gift to others with no strings or expectations attached. You may want to take a moment to reflect on the altruism shown to you by others and by you to others. Many people find that they receive and give few altruistic gifts, and that most of what they do receive or give carries expectations of reciprocity.

There is some evidence that performing altruistic acts benefits the giver, the receiver, and society at large. These acts seem to elevate moods, reinforce self-esteem, give some support for the meaning and purpose for your life, enhance a sense of responsibility, and provide encouragement for both the giver and the receiver. These are also the kinds of outcomes that will aid in your personal growth and development toward becoming the person you want to be, making it easier to cope with your aging self-absorbed parent, who is unlikely to have ever been altruistic.

Let's consider two categories of altruistic acts, collective and individual. Collective altruistic acts are those activities done in conjunction with other people; some good examples are the wide variety of volunteer activities that are available in every community. These are found through particular community organizations, religious groups, social and civic clubs, recreation centers, and so on. These kinds of groups have organized and specific volunteer activities, usually focused on helping others in need, contributing to the community, and providing companionship. They are focused on children, the disabled, the elderly, and others who do not have needed resources. There are rewards for you if you choose collective activities: the support, fun, and companionship that come from the shared experiences and the inner pleasure you feel from giving of yourself to others and seeing that it made a difference. Individual altruistic acts are those you perform to and for other individuals freely and without expectations of their giving back anything to you. These can be simple acts of kindness—onetime acts for one person at a particular time—and may be cost-free. The core principles are that the act is a gift of yourself, there is no hidden motive or expectation, and the receiver does not owe you anything. The following exercise illustrates how to develop such individual acts.

Exercise 11.3: Acts of Altruism

Materials: A tin or small box to hold 2½ by 3½–inch cards; ten to fifteen artist trading cards or a set of playing cards, or cardstock cut to the size; collage materials such as cardstock, patterned paper, dictionary, newspaper, or magazine pages, a variety of stickers, glue, scissors, double-sided tape, and fine sandpaper if using playing cards; a pen for writing, or computer-generated phrases for the cards; paper and other materials to decorate the outside of the tin or box. Optional: an ink pad in your choice of color.

Procedure:

1. Gather all of the materials and find a suitable place to work where you will be free from distractions and interruptions. Determine the number of cards that will fit in the tin or box. If you are using playing cards, use the sandpaper to rough up the parts of the card where you intend to glue or tape.

2. You will have a construction on both sides of the card, the word side and the collage side. Choose one of the following to create the word side of the card:

    ■ Think of an altruistic act that you want to do.

    ■ Write your altruistic acts on strips of paper or use the computer-generated phrases and then paste or tape one on each card.

    Following are some altruistic acts:

    ■ Say hello to someone who looks sad.

    ■ Smile at a child.

    ■ Listen to someone who has a concern, but don't offer advice; just listen.

    ■ Provide needed information.

    ■ Weed a neighbor's flower bed.

- Babysit for a parent who is single or whose spouse is deployed on a military mission.

- Visit and talk with a shut-in or elderly person.

- Play a game (video or board) with a child.

- Help with homework.

- Send a thinking-of-you e-mail to someone who is experiencing adversity.

- Write a letter or card to an active-duty military person.

- Read a story to a child.

- Give a compliment to someone.

- Hug a family member.

You can probably think of other acts.

After you write, glue, or paste the acts on separate cards, you can embellish these, if you like, with stickers, drawings, or cutouts.

3. Turn each card over and create a collage on the other side, either by drawing things, or using other images. You can do what you choose. Here are some ideas:

- Cut or tear a dictionary or newspaper scrap to fit the card, leaving a small border around the scrap. Glue or tape the scrap to the card. Place a large sticker or several small stickers on the scrap, or use an image of your choice. You can repeat these steps using patterned paper.

- Tear an irregular small strip of patterned paper to fit across the bottom of the card and glue it down. Place an image or collection of images on the card and on top of the paper.

- Cut out several small shapes from cardstock in various colors. Glue these to the card in any configuration you choose, even piling some on top of other shapes.

- Cut or tear a wide strip of newspaper to fit down one side of the card. Either cut out a shape (I like hearts), or use a sticker, or find an image to place in the center of the card, slightly overlapping the newspaper strip.

4. Once your cards are complete, you can use the ink pad, if you like, to ink the edges of the card. Hold the card in one hand and the ink pad in the other hand, and slide the card down all edges to ink it.

5. Place the cards in the tin or box. Select one each day to remind yourself of what you can do to be altruistic.

This can be particularly helpful on days when you feel down, or when it seems that nothing is going right.

Recognize and Achieve Positives in Your Everyday Life

Resolve to find a minimum of three positives every day. Positives are simple things that can be inspirational, lift your spirits and mood, and provide hope that you can and will succeed and thrive. Positives such as the following can be used:

What went well. Encountering mainly green lights on the commute to work; a positive medical report.

Avoiding aggravation. A dreaded meeting that was cancelled.

Unexpected beauty. Flowers in bloom; a row of trees with changing leaves.

Wonder. A duck swimming in a puddle in a parking lot; seeing art or dance or athleticism.

Pleasant sensations. Music, tasting a brownie, smelling baking bread, seeing the waves at the beach, or feeling a silk scarf on your neck.

Other. Hearing from a friend with whom you'd lost contact, receiving an unexpected hug from someone you like, or completing a difficult task.

There could be many different varieties of positives that you could experience that are simple and low or no cost, that bring a smile or a flush of pleasure, and that are enriching.

Take a moment to reflect on your experiences today to this moment. Can you identify one to two positives?

There may be two tendencies that you have, as most people do. The first is to focus on the high points, such as receiving a raise or a bonus. The second is to overemphasize the lows, such as having an argument with your spouse or partner. These are common tendencies and are about important events in your life, and I don't want to downplay or minimize these at all. That said, even though the rush is not as high, there can still be an elevation of positive feelings when experiencing little pleasures that are the positives. The next exercise can help you recall some of these.

Exercise 11.4:   Simple Pleasures

Materials: A sheet of paper; a pen or pencil; a set of crayons, colored pencils, or felt markers; and a small notebook

Procedure

1. Find a suitable place to work and sit in silence for one to two minutes. During this time, let your mind wander to the previous week or month, and recall the moments where you felt pleasure. These may have been few or fleeting, but you do remember them.

2. List all of the pleasurable moments you recall on the sheet of paper. These do not have to be in any particular order.

3. Now, repeat step 1 and recall a period of time in the more distant past where there were pleasurable moments or times. You can go back as far as you want to for this step. Add these to the list you developed in step 2.

4. Using the crayons, colored pencils, or felt markers, select five colors to depict each of the following intensities: extremely pleasurable, very pleasurable, somewhat pleasurable, fairly pleasurable, and pleasurable. Review your list of pleasurable events, and highlight each item with the color that depicts its intensity. (For example, I would use yellow to highlight the extremely pleasurable moments or events, bright green for very pleasurable, orange for somewhat pleasurable, bright blue for fairly pleasurable, and aqua for pleasurable.)

5. Review your highlighted list and make a notation beside each extremely or very pleasurable item that you could repeat at this time or in the future. Some may be onetime events, such as hitting a home run in Little League.

6. Use the notebook to record the list of possible pleasureable moments, including any whose intensities are somewhat pleasurable, fairly pleasurable, or just pleasurable.

7. You now have a notebook with possibilities, and you can remind yourself to notice pleasurable things. Use the remainder of the notebook pages to record three pleasurable things every day for a month or longer.

At the end of a month of recording positives, reflect on what the effect has been on your mood, feelings about yourself, and general overall well-being since you began paying attention to the positives in your life.

Even if you are experiencing adversity, you can find that you are better able to manage your feelings and well-being when you give even a minimal focus to the simple pleasures that are positives.

Handle Adversity

However you choose to manage adversity, it will be more advantageous to not involve your self-absorbed parent in your efforts. Go back to chapter 1 and reread the material on the possible effects of aging on your parent. Many of these effects are likely to be what your self-absorbed parent is experiencing; he is likely to have or to show even less empathy for you and is also likely to say and do things that are demeaning or denigrating or dismissive to show your inferiority, and the result is that you can feel worse about yourself. Even if financial assistance would be helpful, in the long run you may be better off finding another way to obtain the financial help you need, or you can reevaluate the necessity for financial assistance.

How do you manage adverse circumstances now? Do you panic and become very anxious and upset? Cry and look to others for solace? Retreat into yourself and become closed off? Seek consultation with others to get their solutions to your concerns? Pray or meditate? Try to think it through? Become depressed or angry? Sulk? Blame others? Criticize yourself? Expect others to fix it? You may find that you do more than one of the items on the list, and that some of these can be effective while others are less so.

Adversity, for this discussion, is not conceived as a crisis where immediate action needs to be taken to prevent or address harm to yourself or to others. *Adverse circumstances* are defined as events that affect you and your family's well-being, that are not usually under your control, and that can have a long-term effect, are not easily addressed, and may produce negative feelings or doubt about your self-efficacy. Examples for adverse circumstances include acute or chronic illnesses, unemployment, military deployment, loss of income, accidents, being the victim of violence, home loss or foreclosure, divorce, death of a loved one, and other such events. Your flawed judgment or decisions may have contributed to the adversity for some of these, but many were not under your control—life happened.

Each person can experience and react to adversity in different ways; no two situations are the same, and the suggestions here for handling adversity are general. Use these as a guide to developing your own unique approach for your unique adversities. Flexibility, a willingness to adjust when needed, and self-understanding are also personal characteristics that can help you. Think about using one or more of the following suggestions.

- Do not panic, as this is not helpful for you or for anyone else. If circumstances seem overwhelming at the time, mentally schedule your thirty-second rant or freak-out for six months in the future. You can yell, cry, stomp around, throw (soft) things, jump up and down, and rail at the universe at that time, but not right now.

- Allow yourself a brief period for mourning, as adversity usually involves a loss. During this brief period, you can quickly go through the stages of grief, where you are shocked, in disbelief, become angry, seek to bestow blame, and can finally come to acceptance. Anger and blame are not helpful to you or to your family, and it is best that you not get stuck there.

- Use problem-solving techniques and skills. First, understand the major problem for the adversity. For example, in the case of an acute illness, the problems could be obtaining diagnosis and treatment, getting insurance approval for procedures, paying for needed medication, and the like. Each adverse situation is different, so understanding the problem is an important task. Second, decide what needs to be done immediately, in the short term and for the long term, and then set priorities for what you need to do. Third, obtain needed information and resources. The final step is to initiate actions based on the first three steps.

- Think about what can be done to lessen the distress for yourself and others who may be impacted, and follow through. Listening, or having someone listen with understanding, is one of the most helpful acts, whether it's you or someone else who is listening. An absence of blame and criticism is also of help. Continue to follow as much of your normal routine as is possible. Routine can also be comforting. Obtaining outside help, such as counselors, clergy, or social agencies, can also be of assistance.

- Involve the family as much as possible. Involving your family provides transparency, enhances communication, strengthens bonds and connections, provides reassurance for spoken and unspoken fears, and can even allow for additional initiatives and ideas.

The final suggestion is to mentally have a plan for handling adversity. You can visualize a plan for handling adversity. The suggestions in this section provide a framework for your plan: manage your emotions, allow yourself a mourning period, use problem-solving techniques and skills, obtain needed resources, involve your family, and mentally develop a plan.

Achieve Balance

Whatever your age is currently, your life is probably busy with many internal and external demands, and you may find it difficult to try to balance all of these. It can feel as though you were always having to attend to crises, to multiple competing demands and expectations, while also trying to meet your personal needs. Let's step back for a moment and see what your current needs and expectations are.

Exercise 11.5:   Needs and Expectations

Materials: Several sheets of paper and a pen or pencil, or a suitable digital device

Procedure:

1. Find a place to work where you will not be disturbed or distracted. Read through all of the instructions before beginning to work.

2. Sit in silence, close your eyes, reflect on your life at the current time, and allow an image of your life to emerge. Do not try to edit or evaluate the image. Just allow it to emerge.

3. When you are ready, open your eyes and write a brief description of your image, noting its shape, colors, size (large, medium, small), an estimate of its weight, any movement (if that is important), and the feelings that you experienced as you visualized your current life.

4. Next, list the following categories, leaving enough room between them to write additional thoughts: current family, work, home,

health, social or recreational, hobbies, and family of origin. You may want to have subcategories for some of these, such as naming each current family member under "current family." List any subcategories at this point.

5. Go back to your image in step 2, and now estimate the overall percentage of your time, effort, and thoughts you expend for each of the categories in step 4. Then distribute that percentage over the subcategories under that category to add up to the percentage for the category. For example, "home" could assume 30 percent of your time, and the distribution of time for home is divided like the following: *Home (30 percent: cleaning 7 percent; repairing 2 percent; decorating 2 percent; lawn and garden 1 percent; meals 18 percent).*

6. Review the percentages for each major category, and write a brief statement about your satisfaction with the percentage of time allocated for each. As an example, you could be very satisfied with the percentage of time spent on social or recreational activities, but not as satisfied with the percentage of time spent on your current family. Note where your time and efforts are overused or underused.

7. If you are satisfied with the balance in your life, you can stop at this point. If you are not satisfied with the balance, make a new list of actions you can do more of, eliminate, or reduce for the categories you want to change. These should be realistic and possible actions.

It is not always easy to achieve balance in your life, as there are external circumstances, unanticipated events, disasters, and crises that affect what you are able to do. You can also face shifting priorities because of matters not under your control. However, in spite of the many constraints and barriers, you can have a more balanced life when you stay focused on your goals and priorities, recognize what you can and cannot do or influence, and manage your emotions. It may not be easy, but don't become discouraged, because you can achieve balance in spite of everything that seems to be working to prevent that from happening.

What are some of the rewards for having balance in your life? You can achieve the following:

- Stronger and more meaningful relationships

- Greater self-confidence and self-efficacy

- Less self-doubt, self-criticism, and the like

- An enhanced ability to manage negative emotions and to experience positive ones

- Increased productivity and performance

- More opportunities to experience calmness and serenity

- Time to focus on the important aspects of your life, thus producing greater satisfaction

- Feelings of being centered and grounded

There are numerous rewards for achieving balance in your life.

Let's end with your image of balance. Close your eyes, breathe deeply, and allow an image to emerge as you think of balance. Don't edit or change what emerges; just let it come. What was your image? I've done this a number of times and have visualized two different images. One image has me sitting on an exercise ball, where I successfully juggle a variety of colorful objects, and in the other image I sit peacefully on a hill looking into the distance.

SUMMARY

This chapter focused on specific actions you can take to survive and thrive in spite of the effects on you of past negative experiences with your self-absorbed parent, his current distressing behaviors and attitudes toward you and your family, and the possible effects of aging on the parent. Suggestions included letting go of emotional baggage that is not positive or helpful in your current life. This was not a call to forgive and forget. Although forgiveness has been shown to have positive benefits, it has to be something that comes from within you and is not something that is imposed or demanded by external sources. What is proposed here are some suggestions for enhancing your self, your closest and most meaningful relationships, and your life. You cannot change the past or your parent. You do have the power and resources to change your self, to grow and develop in positive ways, and to better manage the relationship and interactions with your aging self-absorbed parent. My best to you.

Nina W. Brown, EdD, LPC, received her doctorate from the College of William and Mary, and is a professor and eminent scholar of counseling at Old Dominion University in Norfolk, VA. She is former president of the Society of Group Psychology and Group Psychotherapy, and a current commissioner for the American Psychological Association's Commission on Accreditation. Brown is the author of twenty-seven books on group therapy and narcissism, including *Children of the Self-Absorbed*, *Loving the Self-Absorbed*, and *Whose Life is it Anyway?*

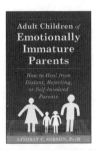